Passing Assessments for the Award in Education and Training

Ann Gravells

Los Angeles | London | New Delhi
Singapore | Washington DC

Learning Matters
An imprint of SAGE Publications Ltd
1 Oliver's Yard
55 City Road
London EC1Y 1SP

SAGE Publications Inc.
2455 Teller Road
Thousand Oaks, California 91320

SAGE Publications India Pvt Ltd
B 1/I 1 Mohan Cooperative Industrial Area
Mathura Road
New Delhi 110 044

SAGE Publications Asia-Pacific Pte Ltd
3 Church Street
#10–04 Samsung Hub
Singapore 049483

Editor: Amy Thornton
Development editor: Jennifer Clark
Production controller: Chris Marke
Project management: Deer Park Productions,
    Tavistock, Devon, England
Marketing Manager: Catherine Slinn
Cover design: Wendy Scott
Typeset by: C&M Digitals (P) Ltd, Chennai, India
Printed and bound by: CPI Group (UK) Ltd,
    Croydon, CR0 4YY

MIX
Paper from
responsible sources
FSC
www.fsc.org   FSC® C013604

© Ann Gravells 2013

First published by Learning Matters SAGE 2013

Apart from any fair dealing for the purposes of research
or private study, or criticism or review, as permitted
under the Copyright, Designs and Patents Act, 1988, this
publication may be reproduced, stored or transmitted in
any form, or by any means, only with the prior permission
in writing of the publishers, or in the case of reprographic
reproduction, in accordance with the terms of licences
issued by the Copyright Licensing Agency. Enquiries
concerning reproduction outside those terms should be
sent to the publishers.

Library of Congress Control Number: 2013946207

British Library Cataloguing in Publication data

A catalogue record for this book is available from the
British Library

ISBN: 978-1-4462-7436-1
ISBN: 978-1-4462-7437-8 (pbk)

CONTENTS

ACKNOWLEDGEMENTS

I would like to give special thanks to the following people who have helped me with this edition of the book. They have freely given their time, knowledge and advice which has resulted in some excellent contributions.

Angela Faulkener
Jacklyn Williams
Mac Macdonald
Mel Page
Peter Adeney
Vic Grayson

I would also like to thank the following people who have supported me with previous editions of this book.

Kathy Beevers
Mel Page
Richard Malthouse
Suzanne Blake
Warwick Andrews

Special thanks also go to my father Bob Gravells who is so good at proof reading and pointing out my typing errors.

I would like to thank my editor Jennifer Clark for her continued support and excellent guidance.

I would especially like to thank Amy Thornton from Learning Matters (which is now part of SAGE Publications Ltd) for her advice, encouragement and tremendous patience with all my questions, e-mails and telephone calls.

Particular thanks go to readers of previous editions of this book who have taken the time to give valuable feedback, which has greatly assisted me when preparing this edition. Also to the Learning and Skills Improvement Service (LSIS) for the unit content used within each chapter. Sadly, LSIS will no longer be operational when this book is printed.

Every effort has been made to trace the copyright holders and to obtain their permission for the use of copyright material. The publisher and author will gladly receive any information enabling them to rectify any error or omission in subsequent editions.

Ann Gravells
www.anngravells.co.uk

AUTHOR STATEMENT

Ann is a director of her own company *Ann Gravells Ltd*, an educational consultancy based in East Yorkshire. She specialises in teaching, training and quality assurance for the Further Education and Skills Sector.

Ann creates resources for teachers and learners such as PowerPoints and handouts for the Award in Education and Training, as well as other qualifications. These are available via her resource website www.anngravells.co.uk/resources

Ann is a consultant to the University of Cambridge's Institute of Continuing Education. She has worked for several Awarding Organisations producing qualification guidance, policies and procedures, and carrying out the external quality assurance of teacher training qualifications. She has been teaching in further education colleges since 1983.

Ann holds a Masters in Educational Management, a PGCE, a Degree in Education, and a City & Guilds Medal of Excellence for teaching. Ann is a Fellow of the Institute for Learning and holds QTLS status.

She is often asked how her surname should be pronounced. The 'vells' part of Gravells is pronounced like 'bells'.

She is the author of:

- *Achieving your Assessment and Quality Assurance Units (TAQA)*
- *Delivering Employability Skills in the Lifelong Learning Sector*
- *Passing PTLLS Assessments*
- *Passing Assessments for the Award in Education and Training*
- *Preparing to Teach in the Lifelong Learning Sector*
- *Principles and Practice of Assessment in the Lifelong Learning Sector*
- *The Award in Education and Training*
- *What is Teaching in the Lifelong Learning Sector?*

She is co-author of:

- *Equality and Diversity in the Lifelong Learning Sector*
- *Passing CTLLS Assessments*
- *Planning and Enabling Learning in the Lifelong Learning Sector*
- *The Certificate in Education and Training*
- *Passing Assessments for the Certificate in Education and Training*

She has edited:

- *Study Skills for PTLLS*

The author welcomes any comments from readers; please contact her via her website www.anngravells.co.uk

In this chapter you will learn about:

- the structure of the book and how to use it
- self assessment activities and guidance for evidencing achievement
- the Award in Education and Training
- assessment methods and activities for the Award in Education and Training
- referencing work
- study skills

The structure of the book and how to use it

The book is designed to help you assess the skills and knowledge you already have, in preparation for your formal assessments towards the Award in Education and Training. It is not a text book, but a self assessment book, and should therefore be read in conjunction with an appropriate text book such as *The Award in Education and Training (Revised 2014)* by Ann Gravells. Reading the book may prove valuable in helping you increase your knowledge and understanding of teaching and training in the Further Education and Skills Sector.

This book will suit anyone taking the Award in Education and Training, whether as a short intensive programme of study, by attending a formal programme over a number of days or weeks, or by taking a distance, open, online or blended learning approach. It is possible to achieve the Award by using units from the Learning and Development qualifications; however, these are not covered as part of this book.

Chapters 1–12 contain self assessment activities for you to carry out, together with guidance to help you demonstrate and evidence your achievement towards each learning outcome of the Award. The book is not intended to give you the answers to questions you may be asked in any formal assessments; your responses will be *specific to you*, the *subject* you will teach and the *context* and *environment* in which you will teach. The Award's units are made up of *learning outcomes* and *assessment criteria* which are listed in each chapter. Learning outcomes are what you *will learn to do*, i.e. obtaining the required skills, knowledge and understanding, and assessment criteria are what you *can do*, i.e. putting it all into practice.

Chapter 13 will help you plan and prepare for your micro-teach session. You will also gain information regarding giving and receiving feedback, and how to evaluate your own session.

At the end of Chapters 1–12 is a completed assessment grid. Each one gives examples of evidence you could provide for the assessment criteria. Evidence can be cross-referenced between the assessment criteria as there is some duplication between the units. The Award consists of three units, which can be achieved independently of each other or at the same time. While the assessment grids will give guidance regarding each separate assessment criterion, you might be assessed more holistically, i.e. towards several of the assessment criteria during the same occasion.

For the purpose of this book, the generic term *teacher* is used, even though you might be called something different: for example, *assessor, coach, counsellor, facilitator, instructor, lecturer, mentor, presenter, staff development manager, supervisor, trainer* or *tutor*. The generic term *learner* is also used and refers to other terms such as *apprentice, candidate, participant, pupil, student* and *trainee*.

Appendix 1 contains a list of relevant educational abbreviations and acronyms, Appendix 2 contains a glossary of terms which relate to the Further Education and Skills Sector, and Appendix 3 shows the structure of the different units which can make up the Award in Education and Training.

The index at the back of the book will help you to locate relevant topics quickly.

Some of the regulations and organisations referred to in this book may only be relevant in England.

Self assessment activities and guidance for evidencing achievement

As you progress through your programme of study, you can work through the self assessment activities in Chapters 1–12. Once you have completed the activities in the first part of each chapter, check your responses with the guidance in the second part of the chapter.

Each chapter relates to one of the 12 learning outcomes of the three units of the Award. Responding to these activities will help you focus upon the assessment criteria and guide you towards evidencing the requirements of the units. The activities will address each individual assessment criterion of the units; however, you might be able to achieve several at the same time depending upon how you will be assessed.

As you work through the self assessment activities, make sure your responses are *specific to you* and the *subject* you will teach. You should state the *context* and *environment* in which you will teach. Examples of the context could be:

- adult education
- armed, emergency and uniformed services
- charitable organisations
- community education
- further education colleges
- higher education institutions and universities
- immigration and detention centres
- on site learning centres

- prisoner and offender centres
- private sector learning
- probation services
- public sector learning
- schools and academies
- sixth form colleges
- voluntary sector learning
- work-based learning

Examples of the environment include classrooms, community halls, outdoor spaces, training rooms, workshops, the workplace, and anywhere else where learning can occur.

If you are currently teaching, you could also explain the documentation you use at work along with the relevant policies, procedures and guidelines you follow. You could write a short case study of how you have demonstrated applying theory to practice, just make sure you anonymise it by not using any names of organisations or learners.

The Award in Education and Training

The Award in Education and Training is an introductory teaching qualification achievable at level 3 on the Qualifications and Credit Framework (QCF), which roughly equates to Advanced (A level) study. You will find more information on the QCF in the next section of this chapter. As it's an introductory qualification it will give you a good idea of how you can teach your subject. You can then take a further teaching qualification if required. The Award is ideal if you are not yet in a teaching role, have just started teaching, or just want to know what the teaching role involves.

The qualification is made up of different units to the value of 12 credits. Think of one credit as approximately 10 hours of learning, therefore 12 credits equates to 120 hours of learning. This will consist of a certain amount of *contact time* with a teacher, such as attending sessions and being assessed. It also consists of your own time, known as *non-contact time,* which can be used for reading, research, completing assignments and gathering evidence of work towards meeting the requirements of the qualification.

The level 3 Award is made up of the following three units (which total 12 credits):

- Understanding, roles, responsibilities and relationships in education and training (3 credits)
- Understanding and using inclusive teaching and learning approaches in education and training (6 credits)
- Understanding assessment in education and training (3 credits)

However, it is possible to achieve part of the Award by taking units from the Learning and Development qualification. These units are known as *accepted equivalents*, but they are only for those who are currently in a teaching and assessing role with learners of their own.

Everyone must take the first Award unit of *Understanding roles, responsibilities and relationships in education and training* which is classed as a *mandatory unit.*

You could substitute the Award unit *Understanding and using inclusive approaches in education and training* with one of the following units from the level 3 Learning and Development qualification:

- Facilitate learning and development for individuals (6 credits) OR

- Facilitate learning and development in groups (6 credits)

You could also substitute the Award unit *Understanding assessment in education and training* with the following unit from the level 3 Learning and Development qualification:

- Understanding the principles and practices of assessment (3 credits).

Appendix 3 shows the structure of the different units which can make up the Award.

If you wish to substitute any units, you will need to discuss this with the organisation you are taking the Award with, as they might only offer the three main units of the Award and not the Learning and Development units.

You will need to ensure that your English, maths and information and communication technology (ICT) skills are of a good quality. You won't want to be making mistakes in front of your learners as this will give a bad impression to them.

As part of the Award, you will need to deliver a short *micro-teach* session to your peers (usually 15 or 30 minutes), or if you are currently teaching, you might be observed with your own learners. Chapter 13 will give you lots of information to help you with this.

The Award can be delivered in different ways depending upon where you choose to take it. For example, a series of evening classes, daytime classes or an online course.

How you are assessed towards achievement of the Award will differ depending upon whom you are registered with. The organisation you are taking the qualification with will register you with an awarding organisation (AO). Each AO will specify how you will be assessed, for example, assignments, case studies, written work and projects. Some might have a more academic focus, i.e. require formal writing and the use of research and referencing. You will need to find out how you will be assessed before you commence, to ensure you can meet the requirements. While the delivery and assessment methods might differ, the content of the qualification units will be the same no matter whom you are registered with.

If you are currently teaching, this is known as *in-service*, and if you are not yet teaching, this is known as *pre-service*. Throughout your career, you might be known as a *dual professional,* i.e. a professional in the *subject* you will teach, as well as a professional *teacher*.

Qualifications and Credit Framework

The Qualifications and Credit Framework (QCF) is a system for recognising skills and qualifications by awarding credit values to units of qualifications in England and

Northern Ireland. The equivalent for Scotland is the Scottish Credit and Qualifications Framework (SCQF), and for Wales the Credit and Qualifications Framework for Wales (CQFW).

These credit values enable you to see how long it would take an average learner to achieve a unit. For example, the *Understanding roles, responsibilities and relationships in education and training* unit of the Award is 3 credits which equates to 30 hours. These hours include *contact time* with a teacher and assessor, and *non-contact time* for individual study and assignment work.

There are three sizes of qualifications in the QCF, each with a title and associated credit values:

- Award (1 to 12 credits)
- Certificate (13 to 36 credits)
- Diploma (37 credits or more)

All qualifications in the QCF use one of the above words in their title, for example, the *Level 2 Certificate in Women's Hairdressing*, the *Level 3 Award in Education and Training*, or the *Level 4 Diploma in Accounting*. The level of the qualification defines how *difficult* it is to achieve and the credit value defines how *long* it will take to achieve.

You don't have to start with an Award, progress to a Certificate and then to a Diploma as all subjects are different. The terms Award, Certificate and Diploma relate to how *big* the qualification is (i.e. its size), which is based on the total number of credits. For example, a Diploma with 37 credits would equate to 370 hours of learning and is therefore a bigger qualification than an Award with 12 credits and 120 hours of learning. The bigger the qualification, the longer it will take to achieve.

The QCF in England and Northern Ireland has 9 levels; ranging from Entry level through levels 1 to 8, for example, level 3 would be easier than level 5.

A rough comparison of the levels to other qualifications is:

1 – GCSEs (grades D-G)

2 – GCSEs (grade A*-C), Intermediate Apprenticeship

3 – Advanced level (A level), Advanced Apprenticeship

4 – Vocational Qualification level 4, Higher Apprenticeship

5 – Vocational Qualification level 5, Foundation Degree

6 – Bachelors Degree

7 – Masters Degree, Postgraduate Certificate and Diploma

8 – Doctor of Philosophy (DPhil or PhD)

The chapters in this book will help you identify how you can demonstrate your learning to meet the assessment criteria of the three main units of the Award.

Working towards the Award

To start the process of achieving your Award, you will need to enrol at a training organisation, college or other establishment that offers it. If you are currently teaching (in-service), your employer might inform you where you can take it and might also fund it for you. If you are not yet teaching (pre-service), you will need to find out where the Award is offered and apply for a place. A quick search via the internet or a phone call to your local training organisation or college will soon locate these. You might be interviewed (in person or on the telephone) and/or have to complete an application form. At this stage it would be useful to ask any questions or discuss any concerns you might have prior to commencing. You should also undertake an initial assessment, which might involve completing a form or having a discussion with your teacher. This will ascertain if you have any particular learning needs, for example with English or maths, and if you need help with study skills. You should always be honest when asked anything so that you can be appropriately supported throughout your learning experience.

Depending upon where you have enrolled, the provider will explain how the programme will be delivered and assessed. It might be by attending formal sessions on a weekly or daily basis at a certain venue, or a mix of attending sessions combined with self-study materials. Other approaches might involve visiting you in your workplace, supporting you on a one-to-one basis, or a blended learning approach, for example, completing activities online via the internet, or working at home with occasional attendance at group sessions.

You will be allocated a designated teacher (who might also assess your work) who will give you ongoing support, guidance and feedback throughout your time taking the Award. If you don't pass any assessments first time, you should be given the opportunity to discuss them with your assessor and have another attempt. The activities in this book will help you understand the content of the units of the Award and prepare you for the assessments. Please remember they are not a substitute for any formal assessments you will be given.

If you are an in-service teacher, it is good practice to be assigned a *mentor*. This is someone, preferably in the same organisation and subject area as yourself, who will be able to give you ongoing help, support and advice. Your organisation might allocate someone to you, but you may not feel comfortable with this, for example, if it's your line manager. Ideally, you should choose a person who can be objective with their help and advice, yet give you support in your subject area.

As you work through the units' requirements you should be informed regularly of your progress and you should have the opportunity to discuss any issues or concerns you may have. The work you produce towards achieving the assessment criteria of the units will be formally assessed and you will receive feedback regarding your progress and achievement. This feedback should confirm your achievements, or outline any further work you will be required to undertake.

A sample of your work might be *internally* and/or *externally quality assured*. Internal quality assurance (IQA) means someone else who works in the same organisation where you are taking the Award will sample aspects of the assessment process. This is to ensure you have been assessed fairly and that your work has met the qualification requirements. External quality assurance (EQA) means someone from the awarding organisation who issues your qualification certificate might also sample the assessment and internal quality assurance process.

Assessment criteria

All qualifications in the QCF contain assessment criteria. The assessment criteria of each of the Award's units begin with verbs; these are words which describe what you need to do to achieve them. When you are working towards them, you need to ensure you can meet the requirements.

Table 0.1 lists the verbs used in the Award with the action required to meet them. The self assessment activities in this book are based on these verbs.

Table 0.1 Verbs used in the Award in Education and Training units

Verb	Action required
Communicate	Actively engage and involve others, for example, during the micro-teach session. Ascertain information from learners to meet their individual needs.
Compare	State the similarities between topics and point out the differences, for example, compare the strengths and limitations of different teaching and learning approaches.
Describe	Give a detailed account of something, for example, the different agencies or people to refer learners to.
Devise	Create and develop something, for example, a teaching and learning plan for a micro-teach session.
Explain	Describe the facts of something and give detailed examples, for example, the roles and responsibilities of a teacher.
Identify	Give the defining characteristics of something, for example, your own areas for improvement after delivering the micro-teach session.
Justify	Give logical reasons and/or arguments to support decisions, for example, why you used particular teaching and learning approaches during your micro-teach session.
Provide	To give or make available, for example, to give constructive feedback to learners.
Review	Critically assess something, for example, a well-considered evaluation of how effective the micro-teach session was, with examples of what went well, what didn't and why.
Summarise	Give a short account of the main facts of the topics in question, for example, key aspects of legislation relevant to your specialist subject.
Use	Demonstrate the use of something, for example, use teaching and learning approaches, resources and assessment methods during a micro-teach session.

Assessment methods and activities for the Award in Education and Training

Each awarding organisation will design their own assessment strategy for the Award, therefore the methods and activities used to assess you might vary depending upon whom you are registered with. You will need to meet all the learning outcomes and assessment criteria for the units you are taking. This will be by demonstrating your knowledge and understanding, and delivering a micro-teach session.

Your assessor will give you feedback regarding your progress and achievement. You might be able to submit a draft of your work for informal feedback before submitting your final work for assessment. If you don't pass, you will be referred, usually with the opportunity to resubmit.

Some of the assessment methods used for the Award are:

- Assessment grids
- Assignments
- Case studies
- Checklists
- Essays
- Observations
- Online assessments
- Portfolio of evidence
- Professional discussion
- Projects
- Questions – written and oral
- Reflective learning journal
- Self-evaluation and action plan
- Written tasks/statements
- Worksheets

You might be assessed by one or more of the above through several activities. Alternatively you might be assessed *holistically*, i.e. having the opportunity to demonstrate several assessment criteria from different units at the same time. If you are in any doubt as to how you will be assessed, or the target dates for the submission of your work, you will need to talk to your assessor.

The assessment methods are briefly explained here. However, you will need to clarify with your assessor any specific requirements which will relate to you.

Assessment grids

An assessment grid contains all the Award's learning outcomes and assessment criteria for each of the units. You will need to write how you have met the criteria and/or link them to documents and evidence such as your micro-teach plan, resources and self-evaluation form.

It might be possible to meet the requirements of several assessment criteria from different units at the same time. If this is the case, you will be able to cross-reference your work rather than repeat it. For example, your micro-teach plan and resources might demonstrate aspects from other units and assessment criteria. An example of an assessment grid can be seen after each chapter in this book.

Assignments

An assignment should ensure that all the assessment criteria can be met through various tasks or problem solving activities. These might not be in the same order as the Award's assessment criteria; however, you should be able to complete all the requirements as you progress through your programme of study. The assignment will assess your knowledge and how you can apply it, perhaps through answering questions, group discussions, presentations to peers, and completing worksheets. You will need time for self-reflection to consolidate your learning as you progress through the activities. You will be given a target date for completion, and possibly a word count for all written work. Your assessor should give you ongoing feedback and if you don't fully meet the criteria, you should be given the opportunity to have another attempt.

Case studies

A case study usually consists of a hypothetical or imaginary teaching or training event for you to analyse. You can then make suggestions regarding how you would deal with the event, which should relate to the assessment criteria of the Award.

Alternatively, you could write a case study of a real situation that you have encountered as a teacher or trainer, again relating it to the assessment criteria of the Award, but keeping it anonymous by not using any names of organisations or learners.

Checklists

A checklist is a list of aspects that need to be met and achieved which will relate to the assessment criteria of the Award. They can be used by you as a form of self assessment to check your progress so far, or by your assessor to confirm your achievement at a given point. They can be completed and dated when the relevant assessment criteria have been met. Checklists are often used in conjunction with other assessment methods.

Essays

Essays are formal pieces of writing to meet the requirements of the Award. There will usually be a minimum and maximum word count to ensure you remain focused and specific, and you will have a deadline date for submission. You will usually have to word process your work in a professional style; however, if it is acceptable for you to handwrite your responses, make sure your writing is legible and neat. Your assessor should give you guidance as to how to present your work. Always check your spelling, grammar, punctuation and sentence structure. Try not to rely on your computer to check words as it doesn't always realise the context within which you are writing.

Essays often include quoting from relevant text books, websites and journals. How to do this is explained briefly towards the end of this chapter. If you cannot keep to a submission date for any reason, make sure you discuss this with your assessor.

Observations

At some point, you will be observed delivering a session (known as a micro-teach session). After the observation you will receive feedback from your assessor and possibly your peers in the group. This feedback should also be given to you in written form, either electronic or a hard copy. A visual recording might be made of your session which you can view in your own time. This will enable you to see and hear things you weren't aware of, for example, saying *erm* or not using much eye contact with your learners. You need to consider these points and the feedback you received when self-evaluating your delivery. You will also observe your peers when they deliver their micro-teach session and may have the opportunity to provide them with feedback.

While you are taking the Award you may find it useful to arrange to observe your mentor if you have one, or another teacher in the same subject area as yourself. This will help you to see how they plan, prepare, deliver, assess and evaluate their session, which should give you some useful ideas.

Online assessments

An online assessment is where you submit your work via the internet to an assessor. You will either e-mail your work or upload it to a learning portal via a dedicated website. There are many online learning sites available, one of the most popular is known as a virtual learning environment (VLE), which is based on Moodle. Moodle stands for a Modular Object-Oriented Dynamic Learning Environment. These sites also enable you to communicate with your assessor and your peers and to view resources and supporting learning materials.

If you are taking the Award totally via an online programme, you might not meet the assessor who will give you feedback concerning your work. You will therefore need to stay in touch regularly and communicate any issues or concerns to them. This might be by e-mail, telephone or other means. You will still have to deliver a micro-teach session and be observed doing this. You will need to meet all target dates for the submission of your work, or communicate with your assessor if you can't meet a date for any reason.

Online assessment can include *formative* (ongoing) assessment, i.e. obtaining feedback from your assessor regarding a draft submission of your work. This feedback will help confirm if you are making good progress or advise you of areas you need to improve. You could then upload your completed work for *summative* (final) assessment when you have completed it.

Please see the assignments and essays paragraphs for information on how to produce your work.

Portfolio of evidence

A portfolio of evidence contains proof of your achievement towards meeting the assessment criteria. This could be electronic (for example, electronic folders containing various files and documents), or manual (for example, hard copies of documents placed in a ring binder or folder). The documents will include written statements as to how you have met the assessment criteria, along with documents such as your micro-teach plan and your assessor's observation report. When producing a portfolio, consider quality not quantity. If you have re-submitted any work, you will need to include your original work as well as your revised work.

Professional discussion

A professional discussion is a conversation with your assessor in which you will justify how you have achieved the assessment criteria of the Award. Your assessor might verbally explore your knowledge and understanding of the teaching role rather than you having to write it. Having a professional discussion with your assessor is a good way to demonstrate how you have met the assessment criteria if you are having difficulty expressing yourself through written work.

A professional discussion can be used as an *holistic* assessment method, meaning several criteria can be assessed at the same time. Your assessor will prompt you to explain how you have met the requirements and ask to see documents which confirm this. They might make written notes during the discussion and/or make a visual or aural recording (often digitally) of your conversation, if appropriate, which can be kept as evidence of your achievement. Prior to the professional discussion taking place, you should agree with your assessor the nature of the content of the conversation to enable you to prepare in advance. You may need to bring along examples of teaching materials you have prepared and used. When you are having the professional discussion try and remain focused, don't digress but be specific with your responses. At the end of the discussion, your assessor should confirm which assessment criteria you have achieved, and which you still need to work towards.

Projects

A project usually consists of practical activities, which can be carried out individually, in pairs or groups. The activities will be based on the assessment criteria of the Award to assess your knowledge and skills. You should be given a target date for completion, and possibly a word count for any written work. However, if you are completing a project with someone else, your own contributions and achievements will need to be clearly demonstrated. Projects are a useful way of preparing for your micro-teach session. For example, you can plan and deliver a short session to your peers, gain feedback and evaluate how you performed. Projects usually take longer in terms of time than an assignment, and might group several assessment criteria together.

Questions – written and oral

You may need to produce answers to written or oral questions, which will be based around the assessment criteria of the units of the Award.

Please see the assignments and essays paragraphs for information on how to produce written work.

If you have answered a written question and met most but not all of the assessment criteria, your assessor might ask you some oral questions to ensure you have the relevant knowledge and understanding to fill any gaps.

Reflective learning journal

A reflective learning journal is a way of helping you formally focus upon your learning, progress and achievement towards the Award. You might be given a template or a document to complete, or you could write in a diary, a notebook, or use a word processor. When you write, make sure your work is legible as your assessor will need to read and understand it. Try and reflect upon your experiences by analysing as well as describing them and be as specific as possible as to how your experiences have met the assessment criteria. You can reflect upon your experiences as a learner taking the Award, and as a teacher if you currently have learners of your own. You could annotate your writing with the assessment criteria numbers such as 1.1, 1.2, 1.3, etc. to show which criteria you feel you have achieved from the relevant units. Don't just write a chronological account of events, consider what worked well, or didn't work, and how you could do something differently given the opportunity. You will need to make sure you address the verbs of the assessment criteria.

Reflection should become a part of your everyday activities and enable you to look at things in detail that you perhaps would not ordinarily do. There may be events you would not want to change or improve if you felt they went well. If this is the case, reflect as to *why* they went well and use similar situations in future sessions. As you become more experienced at reflective writing, you will see how you can make improvements to benefit your learners and yourself.

Self-evaluation and action plan

A self-evaluation and action plan is normally based on a template or document, which you will complete at the end of your micro-teach session or the Award itself. Your writing should clearly evaluate your progress and achievement regarding how you have met the learning outcomes and assessment criteria. The action plan will help you focus upon the skills, knowledge and understanding required for your personal development in the future. This could be by considering what other programmes you could take, for example, to improve your computer skills, or how you plan to apply for teaching or training positions, and what other books or websites you might access to help with your continuing professional development (CPD).

Written tasks/statements

Written tasks or written statements are a way of demonstrating how you have met the required assessment criteria by giving specific examples. You might address individual questions which directly relate to each of the assessment criteria, or answer one question which addresses several assessment criteria holistically.

Please see the assignments and essays paragraphs for information on how to produce your work.

Worksheets

Worksheets are like handouts and include tasks, activities and/or questions for you to carry out. These can be completed during sessions, or in your own time. Worksheets are often used to check progress and might link several assessment criteria together. After completing them, your assessor will check whether your responses can be used to demonstrate achievement of the relevant assessment criteria and give you constructive feedback.

Referencing work

You might be required to use quotes from relevant sources such as text books, websites and journals when submitting your written work for assessment. This is known as referencing and shows that you have read relevant information and related it to your efforts. If you are required to do this, you will need to check with your assessor which writing style to use, and whether it is mandatory or optional to use it. The *Harvard* system is the style that is generally used and standardises the approach to writing and referencing. However, other styles could be used within your writing, but just make sure you are consistent throughout your work regarding layout and punctuation.

It is important to reference your work to:

- acknowledge the work of other writers, authors and theorists

- assist the reader to locate your sources for their own reference, and to confirm they are correct

- avoid plagiarism (i.e. using the work of others without acknowledging it)

- provide evidence of your reading and research

- use existing knowledge and theories to support your work (whether as a direct quote or paraphrased into your own words)

Referencing a book

When using quotes from different sources, for example, a text book, you need to insert *the author, date of publication* and *page number* after any quotation you have used. The full details of the book can then be included in a *reference list* at the end of your work.

For example, if you are describing ground rules, you could state:

> Ground rules should be agreed at the start of a new programme. They '... help create suitable conditions within which learners (and yourself) can safely work and learn' (Gravells, 2013: 100). It is important to establish these early to ensure the programme runs smoothly. If learners do not feel safe, they might not return again, or their learning could be affected.

Any quote you insert within your text should be within quotation marks, often known as speech marks. The name of the author, the year of publication of the book and the page number should be in brackets directly afterwards. At the end of your work, you should have a reference list in alphabetical order, giving the full details of the book you have quoted from. For example:

Reference list

Gravells, A (2013) *The Award in Education and Training.* London: Learning Matters SAGE.

Before inserting a quote, make sure you understand what the quote means and how it will fit within your writing. It could be that you agree with what the author has said and it supports what you are saying, or it could be that you totally disagree with it. If so, explain why you agree or disagree and if it's the latter, state what you would do differently. You need to write what you think, or what your point of view is.

Throughout your writing, you should refer to different sources and authors where applicable. The organisation you are taking the Award with should be able to give you advice regarding using quotes and referencing your work, and provide you with a reading list of relevant text books.

It is advisable to use a range of sources to develop your knowledge and understanding. Reading more than one book will help you to gain the perspectives of different authors. You don't have to read the book fully, you can just locate relevant topics by using the index at the back of the book. If you have a look at the index at the back of this book, you will see all the topics are listed alphabetically, making it easy for you to locate relevant page numbers.

If the quote is longer than three lines of text, indent the paragraph from both margins. Three dots ... can be used to indicate words you have left out. Always copy the words and punctuation as it is in the original, even if there are spelling mistakes. You can add [sic] after the error to denote you are aware of it. Long quotes are always in single line spacing, quotes of three lines or fewer can be in the line spacing of the main text, for example, double line spacing.

If a quote is not used, but the author is still referred to, it will look like this:

> Gravells (2013) advocates the use of ground rules with learners.

Again, the full book details will go in the reference list.

Referencing a website

The quote would be inserted within your writing in a similar way to a text book quote.

For example:

> There is no one single strategy for creating assessments suitable for learners who have difficulty communicating with others, due to the wide range of conditions and impairments that might lead to such a difficulty (LSIS 2012).

It would look like this in your reference list, along with the date it was accessed:

> Assessment (2012) Learning and Skills Information Service
>
> http://www.excellencegateway.org.uk/node/320 (accessed 16.05.13)

The date you accessed it is important, as web pages often change or are removed.

Referencing an online report

The quote would be inserted within your writing in the same way as a text book quote.

For example:

> Teacher educators have traditionally struggled with convincing learners to work on their portfolios, competing against more traditional assessment demands and the habit of putting the portfolio together at the last minute (Hopper & Sanford 2010: 4).

It would look like this in your reference list, along with the date it was accessed:

Hopper, T and Sanford, K (2010) Starting a program-wide ePortfolio practice in teacher education: Resistance, support and renewal. *Teacher Education Quarterly, Special Online Edition.* http://www. teqjournal.org/onlineissue/PDFFlash/HopperSanfordManuscript/fscommand/Hopper_Sanford.pdf (accessed 16.05.13)

There are other ways of referencing different sources of information and you might like to obtain further information from relevant text books or websites to help you.

Study skills

When studying for your Award, you will need to be prepared to use your own time (known as non-contact time) for activities such as research, reading text books and completing assessments. You will need to be self-motivated and able to dedicate an appropriate amount of time to this. If you can, set aside time in a place you won't be disturbed so that you can focus on what is required. If you are interrupted, distracted, hungry or thirsty when studying, you probably won't be able to concentrate well. You will need to keep to any deadlines or target dates for submitting your assessments. Using a diary to forward plan when these need handing in will help when planning your time.

To help you study effectively, it's useful to know the best ways in which to learn. You will probably have a particular learning preference, a way that suits you best. For example, you might like to watch someone perform a task, and then carry it out for yourself, or you might just want to try it out for yourself first. Most people can be grouped into four styles of learning: visual, aural, read/write and kinaesthetic, known by the acronym VARK. If you have access to the internet, go to www.vark-learn.com and carry out the short online questionnaire. See what your results are for each of V, A, R and K and read how your preference can help you learn more effectively.

If you are attending a taught programme, it would be useful to make notes during your sessions to which you can refer to later. This could be on handouts given by your teacher, or hard copies of a presentation. If you have a laptop or tablet, you could make notes electronically during the session (providing this is acceptable). When making notes, try to remain focused, otherwise you might miss something. You could write quickly by cutting out vowels, for example, *tchr* for *teacher*. You could also cut out small words such as *an, are, at, is* and *the*. Whichever way you take notes, make sure you will know what they mean when you look back at them. If you are reading handouts, text books and/or journals, you might like to use a highlighter pen or underline certain words to draw attention to them. You could also make notes in the margins, but only do this on your own materials, not on ones borrowed from others or libraries.

During attended programmes, you might be required to take part in group work or give short presentations to your peers. Use this as an opportunity to work with others and to gain new knowledge and skills. If you are taking the Award via an online or distance learning programme, you might not meet your teacher or your peers in person. However, you will be able to communicate with them either by e-mail or through an online internet-based system.

You might need support to help you improve aspects such as English and computer skills. There might be support available at the organisation where you are taking the Award, or you could attend other relevant programmes. There are some free online programmes available that you could access and which are listed at the end of this chapter. If you don't have access to a computer at home, you could use one at a local library or internet cafe.

If you are unsure of anything while you are studying, or have any concerns, don't be afraid to ask for help. It's best that you get clarification prior to submitting any work for assessment, in case you have misinterpreted something.

Although this is a very brief guide to study skills, you might like to obtain further information from relevant text books or websites to help you. If you are ever in any doubt, talk to your assessor and ask for advice.

Summary

In this chapter you have learnt about:

- *the structure of the book and how to use it*
- *self assessment activities and guidance for evidencing achievement*
- *the Award in Education and Training*
- *assessment methods and activities for the Award in Education and Training*
- *referencing work*
- *study skills*

Theory focus

References and further information

Directorate of Learning Resources *Harvard Referencing: Student Style Guide*. Sunderland: COSC Press.

Gravells, A (2013) *The Award in Education and Training*. London: Learning Matters SAGE.

Gravells, A (2012) *What is Teaching in The Lifelong Learning Sector?* London: Learning Matters.

Hargreaves, S (2012) *Study Skills for Students with Dyslexia*. London: SAGE Publications Ltd.

Malthouse, R and Roffey-Barentsen, J (2013) *Academic Skills: Contemporary Education Studies*. London: Thalassa Publishing.

Pears, R and Shields, G (2010) *Cite Them Right: The Essential Referencing Guide*. Basingstoke: Palgrave Macmillan.

Roffey-Barentsen, J and Malthouse, R (2013) *Reflective Practice in Education and Training*. London: Learning Matters.

Williams, J (2012) *Study Skills for PTLLS* (2nd Edn). London: Learning Matters.

Websites

Ann Gravells (information and resources) – www.anngravells.co.uk

Awarding Organisations – www.ofqual.gov.uk/for-awarding-organisations

Computer free support – www.onlinebasics.co.uk and http://learn.go-on.co.uk

Credit and Qualification Framework for Wales (CQFW) – www.cqfw.org

Digital Unite – http://digitalunite.com/guides

English and Maths free support – www.move-on.org.uk

Learning preference questionnaire – www.vark-learn.com

Qualifications and Credit Framework (QCF) shortcut – http://tinyurl.com/447bgy2

Online free courses in various subjects – www.vision2learn.net

Post Compulsory Education and Training Network – www.pcet.net

Scottish Credit and Qualifications Framework (SCQF) – www.scqf.org.uk

1 UNDERSTAND THE TEACHING ROLE AND RESPONSIBILITIES IN EDUCATION AND TRAINING

This chapter is in two parts. The first part, *Self assessment activities*, contains questions and activities which relate to the first learning outcome of the Award in Education and Training unit *Understanding roles, responsibilities and relationships in education and training*.

The assessment criteria are shown in boxes and are followed by questions and activities for you to carry out. Ensure your responses are *specific to you*, the *subject* you will teach and the *context* and *environment* in which you will teach.

After completing the activities, check your responses with the second part: *Guidance for evidencing achievement*. This guidance is not intended to give you the answers to questions you may be asked in any formal assessments; however, it will help you focus your responses towards meeting the assessment criteria.

At the end of the chapter is an example of a completed *Assessment Grid*, which gives ideas for evidence you could provide towards meeting the assessment criteria. Evidence can be cross-referenced between units and assessment criteria if it meets the requirements.

Self assessment activities

> 1.1 Explain the teaching role and responsibilities in education and training

Q1 Explain what you consider your role as a teacher will be, and the responsibilities you will have.

> 1.2 Summarise key aspects of legislation, regulatory requirements and codes of practice relating to own role and responsibilities

Q2 What legislation, regulatory requirements and codes of practice must you follow to teach your subject?

Q3 Summarise the key aspects of those you have mentioned.

1.3 Explain ways to promote equality and value diversity

Q4 What do the terms equality and diversity mean?

Q5 Explain how you could promote equality and value diversity with your learners.

1.4 Explain why it is important to identify and meet individual learner needs

Q6 Why is it important to identify the needs of learners and how can you do this?

Q7 List at least four examples of these needs and explain how you could meet them.

Guidance for evidencing achievement

1.1 Explain the teaching role and responsibilities in education and training

Q1 Explain what you consider your role as a teacher will be, and the responsibilities you will have.

Your response could explain that your main role should be to teach or train your subject in a way which actively involves and engages your learners during every session, whether this is in the workplace, in a college or other training environment. However, it's not just about *teaching and training*, it's about the *learning* that takes place as a result. You can teach as much as you wish, but if learning is not taking place then your teaching has not been successful. Therefore you must carry out some form of *assessment to* find this out.

Part of your role should be to help your learners achieve their chosen programme or qualification. This will be by using various teaching, learning and assessment approaches, and taking individual learner needs into account.

You could then explain other roles and responsibilities, some of which are listed here:

- acting professionally and with integrity
- attending meetings
- carrying out relevant administrative requirements
- communicating appropriately and effectively with learners and others
- completing attendance records/registers
- complying with relevant regulatory requirements, legislation, policies and procedures, and codes of practice
- differentiating teaching, learning and assessment approaches and materials
- ensuring assessment decisions are valid, reliable, fair and ethical
- ensuring learners are on the right programme at the right level
- establishing ground rules
- following health and safety, and equality and diversity requirements
- giving appropriate information, advice and guidance where necessary
- helping learners develop their English, maths, and information and communication technology skills
- incorporating new technology where possible
- maintaining a safe, positive and accessible learning environment for learners and others
- maintaining records and confidentiality

- partaking in quality assurance processes

- promoting appropriate behaviour and respect for others

- referring learners to other people or agencies when necessary

- reflecting on own practice and partaking in professional development activities

- standardising practice with others

- teaching and training in an inclusive, engaging and motivating way

- using a variety of assessment types and methods to assess progress formally and informally, and giving feedback to learners

- using appropriate equipment and resources

- using icebreakers and energisers effectively

1.2 Summarise key aspects of legislation, regulatory requirements and codes of practice relating to own role and responsibilities

---

Q2 What legislation, regulatory requirements and codes of practice must you follow to teach your subject?

These will differ depending upon the subject you wish to teach, and the context and environment within which you will teach. However, your response could include a generic list of legislation such as:

- Copyright Designs and Patents Act (1988)

- Data Protection Act (1998)

- Equality Act (2010)

- Health and Safety at Work etc Act (1974)

- Safeguarding Vulnerable Groups Act (2006)

You should then state the regulatory requirements which relate to your specific subject such as:

- Control of Substances Hazardous to Health (COSHH) Regulations (2002) for subjects which include the use of chemicals and hazardous materials

- Food Hygiene Regulations (2006) for subjects which include the use of food

- Health and Safety (Display Screen Equipment) Regulations (1992) for subjects which include the use of computer screens

- Manual Handling Operation Regulations (1992) for subjects which include the lifting and carrying of items

You should then state the Codes of Practice which relate to the organisation in which you will teach, as well as any associations or professional bodies you might belong to, such as:

- acceptable use of information technology
- code of conduct
- environmental awareness
- sustainability
- timekeeping

Q3 Summarise the key aspects of those you have mentioned.

Your response should summarise the ones you have listed, for example: *The Copyright Designs and Patents Act (1988)* relates to the copying, adapting and distributing of materials, which includes computer programs and materials found via the internet. Organisations may have a licence to enable the photocopying of small amounts from books or journals. All copies should have the original source acknowledged.

The Control of Substances Hazardous to Health (COSHH) Regulations (2002) applies if you work with hazardous materials such as those used by hairdressing learners for dying clients' hair. Employers are legally obliged to assess all potential hazards related to the work activity, and employees are required to prevent or adequately control the risks that are identified.

The Code of Practice regarding *Acceptable Use of Information Technology* will be written in a format specific to the organisation. If you can access a copy, you could explain how it ensures that all staff and learners are aware of how information technology should be accessed and used, based on principles of honesty, integrity, and respect for others. The Code of Practice should comply with relevant policies and legislation. However, organisations cannot always protect users from the presence of material they may find offensive.

1.3 Explain ways to promote equality and value diversity

Q4 What do the terms equality and diversity mean?

Your response could state that *Equality* is about the rights of learners to have access to, attend, and participate in their chosen learning experience. This should be regardless of ability and/or circumstances.

Diversity is about valuing and respecting the differences in learners, regardless of ability and/or circumstances, or any other individual characteristics they may have.

You could relate your response to equality of opportunity, which is a concept underpinned by The Equality Act (2010) to provide relevant and appropriate access for the participation, development and advancement of all individuals and groups.

The Equality Act (2010) replaced all previous anti-discrimination legislation and consolidated it into one Act (for England, Scotland and Wales). It provides rights for people not to be directly discriminated against or harassed because they have an association with a disabled person or because they are wrongly perceived as disabled.

To ensure you comply with the Equality Act (2010), you need to be proactive in all aspects of equality and diversity. You should make sure your delivery style, teaching, learning and assessment resources promote and include all learners in respect of the Act's nine *protected characteristics* (known as personal attributes):

- age
- disability
- gender reassignment
- marriage and civil partnership
- pregnancy and maternity
- race
- religion or belief
- sex
- sexual orientation.

You could relate your response to a quote such as: *In the past, equality has often been described as everyone being the same or having the same opportunities. Nowadays, it can be described as everyone being different, but having equal rights* (Gravells, 2013: 60).

Q5 Explain how you could promote equality and value diversity with your learners.

Your response should explain how you could promote equality and value diversity with your own learners. For example, promoting positive behaviour and respect by agreeing ground rules with learners from the start of the programme. Another example is that you would challenge prejudice, discrimination and stereotyping as it occurs. You could use pictures in handouts and presentations which reflect different abilities, ages, cultures, genders and races. You can also help your learners by organising the environment to enable ease of access around any obstacles (including other learners' bags and coats), and around internal and external doors. If you are ever in doubt as to how to help a learner, just ask them.

Incorporating activities based around equality and diversity, and the local community and society within which your learners live and work could help your learners be more understanding and tolerant of each other. Try and have discussions regarding your subject which are based on areas of your learners' interest, i.e. cultural topics, popular television programmes and relevant news stories. Place the focus on them to choose rather than you. This should get them thinking about the concept of equality and diversity in society, and how to be accepting and tolerant of others. Using naturally occurring opportunities to explore aspects such as Ramadan or Chinese New Year will also help your learners appreciate and value diversity.

You could explain how you will ensure all learners have access to learning, not only physical access, but ensuring teaching, learning and assessment materials are suitable. For example, producing resources in different formats, i.e. hard copy and/or electronic.

1.4 Explain why it is important to identify and meet individual learner needs

Q6 Why is it important to identify the needs of learners and how can you do this?

Your response could explain that the importance of identifying needs is to ensure they can be suitably met. Knowing what a learner's needs are will help you provide any necessary help and guidance. This should hopefully result in the learner being effectively supported throughout the learning programme.

You should explain how you can identify the individual needs of your learners. For example, by communicating with the learner prior to them commencing the programme, as part of the initial assessment process, during discussions at the interview stage, or tutorial reviews.

For example, to identify if a learner has dyslexia, you could look for some of the indicators in adults which include:

- a low opinion of their capability
- difficulty filling in forms and writing reports
- difficulty structuring work schedules
- losing and forgetting things
- the tendency to miss and confuse appointment times

If you notice any of these, you could arrange for the learner to take a dyslexia test, the results of which will help you offer appropriate support to meet their needs. Your organisation might be able to arrange this or you could find out further information from the Dyslexia Association's website: www.dyslexia.uk.net

Q7 List at least four examples of these needs and explain how you could meet them.

Your list might include learners requiring support with:

- dyslexia
- English as a second or other language
- financial issues
- health concerns

Your response should then explain how you could meet the learners' needs you have listed, for example, what you would do to support a learner who is dyslexic. You could photocopy handouts on to different coloured paper, pastel often helps, or place handouts in a coloured plastic wallet for them. You could also offer to supply handouts and course materials in electronic format, enabling the learner to view, save and/or print them in a size, font and colour to suit their needs. Rather than singling out the particular learner, you could do the same for all learners.

If you are currently teaching, you could produce a case study of how you have met a particular learner's needs; however, make sure you don't use their name.

Theory focus

References and further information

Ayers, H and Gray, F (2006) *An A to Z Practical Guide to Learning Difficulties.* London: David Fulton Publishers.

Clark, T (2010) *Mental Health Matters for FE: Teachers Toolkit.* Leicester: NIACE.

Farrell, M (2006) *Dyslexia and Other Learning Difficulties.* London: Routledge.

Gravells, A (2013) *The Award in Education and Training.* London: Learning Matters SAGE.

Gravells, A and Simpson, S (2012) *Equality and Diversity in the Lifelong Learning Sector* (2nd Edn). Exeter: Learning Matters.

Powell, S and Tummons, J (2011) *Inclusive Practice in the Lifelong Learning Sector.* Exeter: Learning Matters.

Reece, I and Walker, S (2007) *Teaching, Training and Learning: A Practical Guide* (6th Edn). Tyne & Wear: Business Education Publishers.

Wallace, S (2011) *Teaching, Tutoring and Training in the Lifelong Learning Sector* (4th Edn). Exeter: Learning Matters.

Websites

Dyslexia Association – www.dyslexia.uk.net

Equality and Diversity Forum – www.edf.org.uk

Initial and diagnostic assessment – http://archive.excellencegateway.org.uk/page.aspx?o=BSFAlearning difficulty%2Finitialassess

Equality Act (2010) – www.homeoffice.gov.uk/equalities/equality-act/

Government legislation – www.legislation.gov.uk

Regulatory requirements – http://standards.gov/regulations.cfm

UNIT TITLE: Understanding roles, responsibilities and relationships in education and training
Assessment Grid

Learning outcomes The learner will:	Assessment criteria The learner can:	Example evidence
1. Understand the teaching role and responsibilities in education and training	1.1 Explain the teaching role and responsibilities in education and training	An explanation of the roles and responsibilities of a teacher in education and training, such as: teaching and assessing; acting professionally; carrying out relevant administrative requirements; communicating appropriately; completing attendance records/registers. Your job description if you are currently in a teaching role, which highlights your role and responsibilities.
	1.2 Summarise key aspects of legislation, regulatory requirements and codes of practice relating to own role and responsibilities	A list of legislation, regulatory requirements and codes of practice relevant to your role and responsibilities as a teacher/trainer, such as the: Equality Act (2010); Health and Safety at Work etc Act (1974). A summary of the key aspects of each.
	1.3 Explain ways to promote equality and value diversity	An explanation of what equality and diversity mean. An explanation of how you could promote equality and value diversity with your learners, with examples, such as discussing topics in the news. A summary of the Equality Act (2010) and how it could impact upon teaching, learning and assessment.
	1.4 Explain why it is important to identify and meet individual learner needs	An explanation of why it is important to identify your learners' needs such as to give appropriate support. An explanation of how to identify needs, such as: using initial assessments, interviews and discussions. A list of examples of learners' needs, such as: dyslexia; English as a second or other language; financial issues; health concerns. An explanation of how you could meet these needs. A case study of how you have met a particular learner's needs (anonymised).

2 UNDERSTAND WAYS TO MAINTAIN A SAFE AND SUPPORTIVE LEARNING ENVIRONMENT

This chapter is in two parts. The first part, *Self assessment activities*, contains questions and activities which relate to the second learning outcome of the Award in Education and Training unit *Understanding roles, responsibilities and relationships in education and training*.

The assessment criteria are shown in boxes and are followed by questions and activities for you to carry out. Ensure your responses are *specific to you*, the *subject* you will teach and the *context* and *environment* in which you will teach.

After completing the activities, check your responses with the second part: *Guidance for evidencing achievement*. This guidance is not intended to give you the answers to questions you may be asked in any formal assessments; however, it will help you focus your responses towards meeting the assessment criteria.

At the end of the chapter is an example of a completed *Assessment Grid*, which gives ideas for evidence you could provide towards meeting the assessment criteria. Evidence can be cross-referenced between units and assessment criteria if it meets the requirements.

Self assessment activities

> 2.1 Explain ways to maintain a safe and supportive learning environment

Q8 What do you consider a safe and supportive learning environment to be?

Q9 Explain how you could maintain a safe and supportive learning environment.

> 2.2 Explain why it is important to promote appropriate behaviour and respect for others

Q10 What do you consider to be appropriate behaviour and respect for others?

Q11 Explain why it is important to promote appropriate behaviour and respect for others.

Guidance for evidencing achievement

2.1 Explain ways to maintain a safe and supportive learning environment

Q8 What do you consider a safe and supportive learning environment to be?

Your response could state that all aspects of the learning environment, i.e. *physical*, *social* and *learning*, should be appropriate, accessible, supportive and safe for the subject you will teach and for your learners. Informing your learners how you and the organisation will ensure their safety towards each aspect would help make them feel more comfortable and secure, enabling learning to take place.

Learners need to know they will be safe when they are with you, and that they won't be faced with any danger. For example, equipment and resources should not cause harm, furniture should be properly arranged, heating, lighting and ventilation should be adequate (physical). Safe also relates to learners feeling safe to express their opinions without being ridiculed by others.

Learners should also know that you, their peers and others if necessary, will make their time in the learning environment supportive and productive (social). Supportive also relates to giving appropriate advice and/or referring your learners to others if you can't help them with something.

Your session should have a clear aim with objectives which your learners are aware of. You should convey how your learners will be supported towards progress and achievement (learning). You should also demonstrate inclusion and challenge any inappropriate or anti-social behaviour. Ensuring your learners can have a break, if applicable, and have access to refreshment areas and toilets will help them feel safe and supported in the learning environment.

Your learners need to know that their safety is of paramount importance to you and your organisation and that everyone (including the learner) has a responsibility for this. This information can be communicated to your learners in various ways, i.e., through staff and learner handbooks, marketing materials, induction procedures, learner contracts, tutorial reviews, online and learner focus/involvement groups. You might also need to attend Safeguarding training to ensure you are up to date with relevant requirements. Safeguarding is a term used to refer to the duties and responsibilities that those providing a health, social or education service have to carry out/perform to protect individuals and vulnerable people from harm.

If you are currently teaching, you should find out what the policies are at your organisation and explain how these will ensure your learners are safe and supported.

Q9 Explain how you could maintain a safe and supportive learning environment.

Your response could explain how the physical, social and learning aspects can impact upon each other, in positive and negative ways. For example, if the room you are in is too cold, learners might not be able to concentrate, therefore how could you overcome this? If tables are in rows, learners might not be able to communicate well. If learners are thirsty or hungry they might not pay attention or could lose concentration. While it is your responsibility to ensure the learning environment is safe and supportive, you might not be able to control some aspects such as heating, lighting, ventilation, etc. However, what you can do is ensure your session is interesting, meaningful and engaging to your learners.

Initial and diagnostic assessments could be used to ascertain any particular learner needs or concerns in order to help address them: for example, if you have a learner with dyslexia.

Ways of maintaining a supportive learning environment will include agreeing ground rules, using appropriate icebreakers to help learners feel comfortable, planning your sessions to be inclusive, motivating your learners, encouraging your learners to become actively involved and giving regular guidance, praise and feedback. You could encourage peer support though the *buddy* approach. This enables learners to pair up with someone in the group they feel at ease with. They can then keep in touch with each other between sessions to give encouragement and support.

Keeping records such as a register or record of attendance will prove useful should there be a need to evacuate the building; in some organisations it's a legal requirement. You should also be aware of the accident, fire and emergency procedures within your organisation. The Health and Safety at Work etc Act (1974) makes it your responsibility to report a hazard if you see it. You would need to take into account your organisation's Health and Safety policy and not do anything outside of your own responsibility, such as moving heavy equipment or asking your learners to work with hazardous materials. You might need to carry out *risk assessments* for certain aspects of your role. Some resources, particularly electrical ones, require regular maintenance checks and testing. If you see a label on a resource which shows it hasn't been checked for a long time, you will need to report it to the relevant personnel or department.

If you are currently teaching, you could produce a case study of how you have established and maintained a safe and supportive learning environment for your learners.

> 2.2 Explain why it is important to promote appropriate behaviour and respect for others

Q10 What do you consider to be appropriate behaviour and respect for others?

Your response could explain that behaviour is all about how you and your learners interact with each other in an acceptable way. Respect is about accepting others, not being rude to them or lowering their confidence and self-esteem in any way. You could explain that you would *lead by example* to model good practice. If you demonstrate appropriate behaviour and respect for others, hopefully your learners and others will emulate this. Being a professional involves acting with integrity, behaving in the correct manner for your role, and respecting others as you would wish them to respect you.

Appropriate behaviour and respect for others includes:

- agreeing ground rules with learners
- being honest, reliable and trustworthy

- challenging and managing inappropriate behaviour

- communicating appropriately

- encouraging trust, honesty, politeness and consideration towards others

- ensuring the learning environment is accessible, safe and suitable

- establishing routines

- liaising and working with others in a professional manner

- listening to others' points of view

- not overstepping the boundaries of your role

- planning and preparing adequately

- supporting learners and others as necessary

- treating all learners as individuals and teaching in an inclusive way

- using a variety of inclusive teaching, learning and assessment approaches

- valuing others' opinions and not imposing your own upon them

Your learners should also demonstrate appropriate behaviour during sessions, and respect their peers and others they come into contact with. This should lead to an appropriate atmosphere in which learning can effectively take place.

Q11 Explain why it is important to promote appropriate behaviour and respect for others.

Your response could explain why you feel it is important, for example, if you didn't challenge and manage inappropriate behaviour, your learners might become disruptive and offensive to you and/or other learners. You could explain what you would do in certain situations, for example, if a colleague did something you believe to be unacceptable, you could have a quiet word with them. However, if it is very serious you might need to report them to someone else.

If appropriate behaviour and respect is not established and maintained, disruption will occur and learning might not take place.

If you are currently teaching, you could link your response to your organisation's codes of practice.

Theory focus

References and further information

Appleyard, N and Appleyard, K (2010) *Communicating with Learners in the Lifelong Learning Sector.* Exeter: Learning Matters.

Gravells, A (2013) *The Award in Education and Training.* London: Learning Matters SAGE.

National Institute of Adult and Continuing Education (2007) *Safer Practice, Safer Learning*. Ashford: NIACE.

Vizard, D (2012) *How to Manage Behaviour in Further Education.* London: SAGE Publications Ltd.

Wallace, S (2007) *Managing Behaviour in the Lifelong Learning Sector* (2nd Edn). Exeter: Learning Matters.

Websites

Behaviour tips – www.pivotaleducation.com

Classroom management free videos – www.bestyearever.net/videos/?goback=.gmr_27003. gde_27003_member_196422762

Dealing with behaviour – http://newteachers.tes.co.uk/content/dealing-behaviour-issues-%E2%80%93-guide-new-teachers

Health & Safety at Work etc Act (1974) – www.hse.gov.uk/legislation/hswa.htm

Icebreakers – http://adulted.about.com/od/icebreakerstp/toptenicebreakers.htm and http://www.mwls.co.uk/icebreakers/

Risk assessments – www.hse.gov.uk/risk/fivesteps.htm

Safeguarding – www.education.gov.uk/search/results?q=safeguarding

Risk assessments – www.hse.gov.uk/risk/fivesteps.htm

Safeguarding Vulnerable Groups Act (2006) – www.opsi.gov.uk/ACTS/acts2006/ ukpga_20060047_en_1

**UNIT TITLE: Understanding roles, responsibilities and
relationships in education and training
Assessment Grid**

Learning outcomes The learner will:	Assessment criteria The learner can:	Example evidence
2. Understand ways to maintain a safe and supportive learning environment	2.1 Explain ways to maintain a safe and supportive learning environment	An explanation of what you consider is a safe and supportive learning environment, i.e. how you can ensure the physical, social and learning aspects are appropriate, accessible and free from hazards. An explanation of how you can maintain a safe and supportive learning environment. For example, carrying out risk assessments. Copies of relevant organisation policies and procedures highlighting aspects relating to safety, and support for learners. Records of risk assessments. Records of training attended such as Health & Safety and Safeguarding. A case study of how you have established and maintained a safe and supportive learning environment for your learners (anonymised).
	2.2 Explain why it is important to promote appropriate behaviour and respect for others	An explanation of what you consider appropriate behaviour and respect for others to be, such as interacting and communicating in an acceptable way. An explanation of why it is important to promote appropriate behaviour and respect for others, for example, to create an appropriate atmosphere in which learning can effectively take place. Written examples of ways you could promote appropriate behaviour and respect for others such as: agreeing ground rules; challenging inappropriate behaviour. Copies of relevant organisation codes of practice and/or policies highlighting aspects relating to behaviour and respect.

3 UNDERSTAND THE RELATIONSHIPS BETWEEN TEACHERS AND OTHER PROFESSIONALS IN EDUCATION AND TRAINING

This chapter is in two parts. The first part, **Self assessment activities**, contains questions and activities which relate to the third learning outcome of the Award in Education and Training unit **Understanding roles, responsibilities and relationships in education and training.**

The assessment criteria are shown in boxes and are followed by questions and activities for you to carry out. Ensure your responses are *specific to you*, the *subject* you will teach and the *context* and *environment* in which you will teach.

After completing the activities, check your responses with the second part: **Guidance for evidencing achievement**. This guidance is not intended to give you the answers to questions you may be asked in any formal assessments; however, it will help you focus your responses towards meeting the assessment criteria.

At the end of the chapter is an example of a completed **Assessment Grid,** which gives ideas for evidence you could provide towards meeting the assessment criteria. Evidence can be cross-referenced between units and assessment criteria if it meets the requirements.

Self assessment activities

> 3.1 Explain how the teaching role involves working with other professionals

Q12 List at least four other professionals with whom you might work as part of your teaching role.

Q13 Explain how your role would involve working with the other professionals you have identified.

> 3.2 Explain the boundaries between the teaching role and other professional roles

Q14 Explain at least four boundaries which you might encounter between your teaching role and your other professional roles.

> 3.3 Describe points of referral to meet the individual needs of learners

Q15 List at least four individual needs of learners.

Q16 Describe the points of referral to meet those needs.

Guidance for evidencing achievement

3.1 Explain how the teaching role involves working with other professionals

Q12 List at least four other professionals with whom you might work as part of your teaching role.

Your response should list at least four other professionals with whom you might work with at some point. Your list could include some of the following:

- administration staff
- assessors
- budget holders
- caretakers
- cleaners
- co-tutors
- customers
- external quality assurers
- finance staff
- health and safety officers
- human resources staff
- internal quality assurers
- learning support staff
- managers
- other teachers and trainers
- other training providers
- reprographics staff
- safeguarding officers
- staff development personnel
- supervisors
- support workers
- technicians
- union staff
- work placement co-ordinators

Q13 Explain how your role would involve working with the other professionals you have identified.

Your response should explain how you would work with other professionals, particularly those you have identified in your list.

For example, you should always be polite and professional and treat others with respect. It would be useful to find out and understand a little about the job roles of others, how they can support you, and how you can support them. However, don't feel you need to support them too much by carrying out aspects of their role for them, otherwise you might be blurring the boundary between your role and their role. You should never feel you have to resolve a situation on your own, there should be others who can help when necessary.

Examples of working with other professionals include:

- Administrative staff – communicating with appropriate personnel to ensure that your learners have been registered with the relevant awarding organisation (if applicable). Informing the receptionist of the arrival of visitors so that a visitor's pass, parking, refreshments, etc. can be organised.

- Internal quality assurer – liaising with them regarding the progress of your learners and informing them of your activities so that they can monitor and sample aspects of your work. Listening to their feedback and not taking developmental points personally.

- Learning support staff – arranging support for learners with particular needs such as help with maths or using computers.

- Managers – responding to requests for information and data, attending meetings and contributing towards issues under discussion.

If you are currently teaching, you could produce a case study of how your teaching role has involved working with other professionals.

3.2 Explain the boundaries between the teaching role and other professional roles

---

Q14 Explain at least four boundaries which you might encounter between your teaching role and your other professional roles.

Your response could explain that boundaries are about knowing where your role as a teacher or trainer stops. You should be able to work within the limits of that role, yet follow all relevant policies and procedures.

Examples include:

- Not doing something which is part of someone else's role. For example, if you need to get handouts photocopied and there is a reprographics department, you shouldn't enter their office and make the copies yourself. You need to follow the correct procedures.

- Not blurring the teaching role with your supportive role, i.e. becoming too friendly with your learners. For example, you might feel it sensible to make a telephone call to a learner who has been absent but making regular calls would be inappropriate. Giving your personal telephone number to learners could be seen as encouraging informal contact, and you may get calls or texts which are not suitable or relevant. You might not want to take your break with your learners or join their social networking sites as you could become more of a friend than a teacher. When you are with learners, you need to remain in control, be fair and ethical and not demonstrate any favouritism towards particular learners: for example, by giving one more support than others.

- Not blurring the teaching and assessment roles. For example, you might have taught everything needed for your learners to pass an assignment, but they might not have met the required criteria when submitting it. You should not pass a learner because you like them, or feel they have worked hard. You must remain objective with your decision and not pass them if they haven't fully met the requirements.

- Not putting your professional role under pressure, for example, accepting a learner on to your programme instead of offering them a more suitable programme, just because you need a certain number of learners for it to go ahead. You might have difficult decisions to make as to whether you accept a learner or not. However, if you make a decision not to accept a learner, you will need to justify your reasons.

There are also some common boundaries you should not overstep, i.e. it is unprofessional to use bad language, to touch learners in an inappropriate way or to let your personal problems affect your work.

If you are currently teaching, you could produce a case study of boundaries you have encountered between your roles, and how you have overcome them.

3.3 Describe points of referral to meet the individual needs of learners

---

Q15 List at least four individual needs of learners.

Your response should list the individual needs that your learners might have. Your list could include some of the following:

- access to, or fear of, technology
- alcohol or substance misuse
- childcare concerns
- death in the family
- emotional or psychological problems
- English as a second or other language
- financial issues
- health concerns
- limited basic skills such as English and maths
- transport problems
- unsure which career path to take

Q16 Describe the points of referral to meet those needs.

Your response should describe the points of referral you could recommend to your learners, particularly for those needs you have identified in your list. For example:

- access to, or fear of, technology – local library or internet café, specialist colleagues and/ or training programmes
- alcohol or substance misuse – relevant support agencies, telephone helplines, Citizens Advice Bureau
- health concerns – health centres, general practitioners, hospitals
- unsure which career path to take – National Careers Service, specialist staff within the organisation

You could add the contact details for each, i.e. the names of people, agencies and organisations along with their address, telephone and/or website details.

If you are currently teaching, you could produce a case study regarding points of referral you have used to meet the individual needs of learners.

Theory focus

References and further information

Berry, J (2010) *Teachers' Legal Rights and Responsibilities: A Guide for Trainee Teachers and Those New to the Profession* (2nd Edn). Hertfordshire: University of Hertfordshire Press.

Gravells, A (2013) *The Award in Education and Training*. London: Learning Matters SAGE.

IfL (2008) *Code of Professional Practice*. London: Institute for Learning.

Reece, I and Walker, S (2008) *Teaching, Training and Learning: A Practical Guide* (6th Edn). Tyne & Wear: Business Education Publishers Ltd.

Tummons, J (2010) *Becoming a Professional Tutor in the Lifelong Learning Sector* (2nd Edn). Exeter: Learning Matters.

Websites

Citizens Advice Bureau – www.citizensadvice.org.uk

Database of self help groups – www.self-help.org.uk

Dyslexia Association – www.dyslexia.uk.net

National Careers Service – https://nationalcareersservice.direct.gov.uk/Pages/Home.aspx

**UNIT TITLE: Understanding roles, responsibilities
and relationships in education and training
Assessment Grid**

Learning outcomes The learner will:	Assessment criteria The learner can:	Example evidence
3. Understand the relationships between teachers and other professionals in Education and Training	3.1 Explain how the teaching role involves working with other professionals	A list of other professionals with whom you might work as part of your teaching role such as: administration staff; internal quality assurers; learning support staff; managers. An explanation of how your role would involve working with the other professionals you have identified in your list, for example, communicating information. A case study of how your teaching role has involved working with other professionals (anonymised).
	3.2 Explain the boundaries between the teaching role and other professional roles	An explanation of the boundaries which you might encounter between your teaching role and your other professional roles, such as not blurring the teaching role with your supportive role, i.e. becoming too friendly with your learners. A case study of boundaries you have encountered between your roles, and how you have overcome them (anonymised).
	3.3 Describe points of referral to meet the individual needs of learners	A list of individual needs of learners such as: childcare concerns; financial issues; limited basic skills; transport problems. A description of relevant points of referral and support systems available such as: people; agencies; organisations; websites, etc. to meet the needs you have identified. A case study regarding points of referral you have used to meet the individual needs of learners (anonymised).

4 UNDERSTAND INCLUSIVE TEACHING AND LEARNING APPROACHES IN EDUCATION AND TRAINING

This chapter is in two parts. The first part, **Self assessment activities**, contains questions and activities which relate to the first learning outcome of the Award in Education and Training unit **Understanding and using inclusive teaching and learning approaches in education and training.**

The assessment criteria are shown in boxes and are followed by questions and activities for you to carry out. Ensure your responses are *specific to you*, the *subject* you will teach and the *context* and *environment* in which you will teach.

After completing the activities, check your responses with the second part: **Guidance for evidencing achievement.** This guidance is not intended to give you the answers to questions you may be asked in any formal assessments; however, it will help you focus your responses towards meeting the assessment criteria.

At the end of the chapter is an example of a completed **Assessment Grid,** which gives ideas for evidence you could provide towards meeting the assessment criteria. Evidence can be cross-referenced between units and assessment criteria if it meets the requirements.

Self assessment activities

> 1.1 Describe features of inclusive teaching and learning

Q17 What does the term inclusive teaching and learning mean?

Q18 Describe the features of inclusive teaching and learning.

> 1.2 Compare the strengths and limitations of teaching and learning approaches used in own area of specialism in relation to meeting individual learner needs

Q19 List at least six different teaching and learning approaches that you could use for your subject specialism.

Q20 Compare the strengths and limitations of the teaching and learning approaches you have identified, and explain how they could meet individual learner needs.

> 1.3 Explain why it is important to provide opportunities for learners to develop their English, mathematics, ICT and wider skills

Q21 How could you provide opportunities for your learners to develop their English, mathematics, ICT and wider skills?

Q22 Explain why it is important to do this.

Guidance for evidencing achievement

> 1.1 Describe features of inclusive teaching and learning

Q17 What does the term inclusive teaching and learning mean?

Your response could state that inclusive teaching and learning is about ensuring all learners have the opportunity to be involved and included in the teaching and learning process. You should also take into account any individual learning or support needs. It's also about treating all learners equally and fairly, without directly or indirectly excluding anyone. Inclusion is about attitudes as well as behaviour, as learners can be affected by the words or actions of others. You are not teaching your subject to a group of learners who are all the same, but to a group of individuals with different experiences, abilities and needs, which should be recognised and respected.

Q18 Describe the features of inclusive teaching and learning.

Your response could state that a key feature would be to promote a positive culture of equality of opportunity whereby all learners can attend, participate, feel safe and valued.

You could then describe features of achieving this such as using learners' names when they arrive and when talking to them, using eye contact and speaking personally to them during each session. Another feature is to ask an open question to every learner during each session (ones that begin with *who, what, when, where, why* and *how*). Using the pose, pause, pick (PPP) technique of questioning can be a way of including all your learners. This is where you pose a question, then pause for a few seconds so that all learners are thinking about a response, while you use eye contact with everyone. You can then pick a learner to answer the question, stating their name as you look at them. This is better than stating a learner's name before the question, as the other learners will not be thinking about the answer as they know someone else has been asked. You might need to prepare some questions in advance, or use opportunities which occur during the session.

Other features which you could describe include:

- ascertaining individual needs, learning preferences and goals
- being approachable and accessible, enabling learners to feel comfortable to disclose any concerns
- briefing other staff who are involved with the learner such as learning support assistants
- challenging stereotyping, discrimination and prejudice as it happens
- differentiating activities to address individual differences: for example, different abilities and levels
- encouraging group work where learners can mix and participate with all members of the group over a period of time
- ensuring the environment is accessible to all learners

- identifying where modifications or changes are needed to equipment or activities
- involving all learners at some point during each session
- recognising and valuing individual contributions and achievements
- using self assessment and peer assessment activities
- using starter activities at the beginning of a session, and summary activities at the end which involve everyone
- using a wide range of teaching, learning and assessment approaches based upon learner needs
- using resources and materials which positively promote all aspects of community and society, equality and diversity

You could cross-reference your response to the unit: Understanding and using inclusive teaching and learning approaches in education and training 2.1 if you have met the required criteria.

1.2 Compare the strengths and limitations of teaching and learning approaches used in own area of specialism in relation to meeting individual learner needs

---

Q19 List at least six different teaching and learning approaches that you could use for your subject specialism.

Your list could include some of the following:

- demonstrations
- discussions
- distance or open learning
- e-learning
- explanations
- group work
- instruction
- practical activities
- projects
- presentations
- questions and answers
- research
- role plays
- seminars
- technology-based learning

Your approaches will very much depend upon the *subject* you are teaching, and the *context* and *environment* you are teaching in. However, you should choose approaches that will engage, stimulate and motivate your learners to achieve their full potential.

Q20 Compare the strengths and limitations of the teaching and learning approaches you have identified, and explain how they could meet individual learner needs.

You might like to create a table to compare the approaches you have identified. For example:

Approach	Strengths	Limitations	Meeting individual needs
Demonstrations	Can be supported with handouts and activities to cover all learning preferences. Can increase attention and confidence. Can clearly show a skill.	Equipment may not be available or in working order. Larger groups may not be able to see the demonstration or have enough resources. Individuals may not pay attention, get bored or miss something if it's demonstrated too quickly.	Learners with a visual or hearing impairment can be nearer to the demonstration. Can be paced to suit the learners. Repetition and reinforcement can be carried out to emphasise key aspects. Questioning can be used to check understanding.
Discussions	All learners can participate and share knowledge and experiences.	Some learners may be shy or not want to be involved. Easy to digress. Teacher needs to keep the group focused and set a time limit. Some learners might dominate.	A discussion could help learners express themselves if they struggle with writing. Can involve each learner with prepared questions. A summary can be used to draw out key learning points.
Distance or open learning.	Learning can occur at a time and place to suit the learner. Can be combined with other learning methods, e.g. blended learning.	Could be a long gap between submitting work for assessment and receiving feedback. Self-discipline is needed. Targets must be clearly agreed. Learner may never meet teacher/assessor.	Learners who cannot attend regular sessions can take a programme of learning at times to suit their personal and working life. Self assessment can provide reinforcement of progress and help with motivation. Materials can be differentiated to allow for different learning styles.

Approach	Strengths	Limitations	Meeting individual needs
e-learning	Learning can take place anywhere a computer is available. Learning can be flexible. Ongoing support is given.	Learners need access to a computer and need to be computer literate. Self-discipline is needed, along with clear targets. Authenticity of learner's work may need validating. Technical support may be required.	Learners who struggle with handwritten work can create electronic documents and presentations which can be spellchecked.
Group work	Allows interaction between learners. Learners learn from each other's experiences and knowledge. Encourages participation and variety. Rotating group members enables all learners to work with each other.	Careful management by the teacher is required regarding time limits, progress, and ensuring all group members are clear with the requirements. Potential for personality clashes. One person may dominate. Learners might get left out or be too shy to contribute. Ground rules might be needed to keep the group on track. Time is needed for a thorough de-brief and feedback.	Learners who are shy can help improve their confidence by getting involved and working with others. Self assessment can help individual learners see how they are progressing.
Instruction	If one to one, a good method of pacing learning to suit the individual. Learners can hear and/or see what they should do, and try this out immediately for themselves.	If to a group, some learners may get left behind or forget what to do. Needs supporting with a handout or further information/activities. Appropriate positioning is required, e.g. for left handed learners with right handed teachers.	Can be carried out at a pace which is appropriate, for example, if a learner needs more time to carry out a task.

You could cross-reference your response to the unit: Understanding and using inclusive teaching and learning approaches in education and training 2.2 if you have met the required criteria.

> 1.3 Explain why it is important to provide opportunities for learners to develop their English, mathematics, ICT and wider skills

Q21 How could you provide opportunities for your learners to develop their English, mathematics, ICT and wider skills?

Your response could explain how you could provide developmental opportunities during your sessions, for example, based on:

English: reading, writing, listening, speaking, discussing.

Maths: approximations, estimations, calculations, measurements.

ICT: using smart phones, computers, tablets, laptops, etc. for e-mail, web-based research, social networking, viewing videos, word-processing assignments, using presentation packages for projects, and virtual learning environments (VLE) for accessing and submitting resources and materials.

Wider skills:

Citizenship – discussions based on nationality, politics and the state.

Employability – creating a curriculum vitae (CV) and applying for jobs.

Enterprise – setting up a small business, creating a website and online ordering system.

Social responsibility – timekeeping, personal development, behaviour and professionalism, confidence, health and well being.

Sustainability – how to recycle, reuse and reduce usage.

Q22 Explain why it is important to do this.

Your response could explain that your learners' personal skills, knowledge and understanding will improve as a result. This is important as it will hopefully enable learners to function confidently, effectively and independently in their personal and professional lives. Learners who possess skills in these areas should be able to progress in education, training and employment and make a positive contribution to the communities in which they live and work.

You shouldn't have to be highly qualified with English and maths, but know enough to make it relevant to the subject you are delivering. For example, maths doesn't have to be complex equations, it can be about using numerical skills such as planning a household budget, working out the cost of a shopping list, calculating the amount of paint needed to decorate a room, or comparing gas and electricity prices.

However, you might feel your own skills do need improving, therefore you could partake in further training yourself. If you are not competent you will not set a good example to your learners. For example, if you spell words wrongly in a handout, have difficulty making calculations or can't use a computer, your learners may lose confidence in you.

Theory focus

References and further information

Becta (2009) *Harnessing Technology Review 2008: The Role of Technology and its Impact on Education.* Coventry: Becta.

Gravells, A (2013) *The Award in Education and Training.* London: Learning Matters SAGE.

Haythornthwaite, C and Andrews, R (2011) *e-learning Theory and Practice.* London: Learning Matters.

Hill, C (2008) *Teaching with E-learning in the the Lifelong Learning Sector* (2nd Edn). Exeter: Learning Matters.

Holmes, B and Gardner, J (2006) *e-learning Concepts and Practice.* London: Sage Publications Ltd.

Skills for Business (2007) *Inclusive Learning Approaches for Literacy, Language, Numeracy and ICT.* London: LLUK.

Wallace, S (2011) *Teaching, Tutoring and Training in the Lifelong Learning Sector* (4th Edn). Exeter: Learning Matters.

Websites

Approaches to teaching and learning – www.excellencegateway.org.uk/ page.aspx?o=127654

English and Maths free support – www.move-on.org.uk

Further Education Guide to using learning technology – http://feweek.co.uk/2013/02/22/guide-to-fe-learning-tech/?goback=.gde_4139923_member_217969739

ICT free support – www.onlinebasics.co.uk and http://learn.go-on.co.uk

Inclusive teaching –www.open.ac.uk/inclusiveteaching/pages/inclusiveteaching/index.php

Learning and Skills Network (2008) *Personal Learning and Thinking Skills: Lessons from the wider key skills* http://archive.excellencegateway.org.uk/media/post16/files/keyskillspltspublication.pdf

Online free courses in various subjects – www.vision2learn.net

Online games –www.npted.org/schools/sandfieldsComp/games/Pages/Game-Downloads.aspx

Online presentations – www.prezi.com

Using computers and technology: free guides – http://digitalunite.com/

Using IT – www.reading.ac.uk/internal/its/training/its-training-index.aspx

Using VLEs – www.ofsted.gov.uk/resources/virtual-learning-environments-e-portfolio

Video e-mail – http://mailvu.com/

UNIT TITLE: Understanding and using inclusive teaching and learning approaches in education and training
Assessment Grid

Learning outcomes The learner will:	Assessment criteria The learner can:	Example evidence
1. Understand inclusive teaching and learning approaches in education and training	1.1 Describe features of inclusive teaching and learning	A definition of what *inclusive teaching and learning* means, for example, ensuring all learners have the opportunity to be involved and included in the teaching and learning process. A description of the features of inclusive teaching and learning, such as promoting a positive culture of equality of opportunity whereby all learners can attend, participate, feel safe and valued. *Cross-referenced to the unit: Understanding and using inclusive teaching and learning approaches in education and training 2.1.*
	1.2 Compare the strengths and limitations of teaching and learning approaches used in own area of specialism in relation to meeting individual learner needs	A list of at least six different teaching and learning approaches which you could use for your subject specialism, such as: demonstrations; discussions; group work; projects; presentations; role plays; seminars. A comparison of the strengths and limitations of the teaching and learning approaches you have identified in your list, explaining how they could meet individual learner needs. This information could be displayed as a table with the headings: Approach, Strengths, Limitations, Meeting individual needs *Cross-referenced to the unit: Understanding and using inclusive teaching and learning approaches in education and training 2.2.*
	1.3 Explain why it is important to provide opportunities for learners to develop their English, mathematics, ICT and wider skills	An explanation of how you could provide opportunities for your learners to develop their English, mathematics, ICT and wider skills. For example: English: reading; writing; listening; speaking; discussing. An explanation of why it is important to do this, such as to improve learners' personal skills, knowledge and understanding, as well as their confidence and ability to work effectively and independently.

5 UNDERSTAND WAYS TO CREATE AN INCLUSIVE TEACHING AND LEARNING ENVIRONMENT

This chapter is in two parts. The first part, *Self assessment activities*, contains questions and activities which relate to the second learning outcome of the Award in Education and Training unit *Understanding and using inclusive teaching and learning approaches in education and training.*

The assessment criteria are shown in boxes and are followed by questions and activities for you to carry out. Ensure your responses are *specific to you*, the *subject* you will teach and the *context* and *environment* in which you will teach.

After completing the activities, check your responses with the second part: *Guidance for evidencing achievement*. This guidance is not intended to give you the answers to questions you may be asked in any formal assessments; however, it will help you focus your responses towards meeting the assessment criteria.

At the end of the chapter is an example of a completed *Assessment Grid,* which gives ideas for evidence you could provide towards meeting the assessment criteria. Evidence can be cross-referenced between units and assessment criteria if it meets the requirements.

Self assessment activities

> 2.1 Explain why it is important to create an inclusive teaching and learning environment

Q23 In Chapter 4 (Q17) you described what inclusive teaching and learning meant. In Q18 you described the features of inclusive teaching and learning. Now, explain why it is important to create an environment which is inclusive, to ensure teaching and learning are effective.

> 2.2 Explain why it is important to select teaching and learning approaches, resources and assessment methods to meet individual learner needs

Q24 In Chapter 4 (Q20) you compared the strengths and limitations of the teaching and learning approaches you could use for your subject, and stated how they could meet individual learner needs. Now list three resources and three assessment methods which you could use with your learners, and explain how they could meet individual learner needs.

Q25 Explain why it is important to select appropriate teaching and learning approaches, resources and assessment methods to meet individual needs.

2.3 Explain ways to engage and motivate learners

Q26 What do the terms *engaging* and *motivating* mean?

Q27 Explain how you can engage and motivate your learners.

2.4 Summarise ways to establish ground rules with learners

Q28 What are ground rules and why use them?

Q29 Summarise at least two ways in which you could establish ground rules with your learners.

Guidance for evidencing achievement

2.1 Explain why it is important to create an inclusive teaching and learning environment

Q23 In Chapter 4 (Q17) you described what inclusive teaching and learning meant. In Q18 you described the features of inclusive teaching and learning. Now, explain why it is important to create an environment which is inclusive, to ensure teaching and learning are effective.

Your response could explain that an inclusive environment is important for effective teaching and learning to take place. You must ensure all individual learners are included in all activities. If any learners are excluded for any reason, they might not feel involved and therefore not learn effectively. The environment includes not only the venue, equipment and resources used, but also your attitude and the support you give to your learners. While learning can take place almost anywhere, not all environments will be totally suitable; however, it's *how* you deliver and assess your subject that will lead to effective inclusive learning. If you can convey passion and enthusiasm, you will help motivate your learners to want to learn more.

To be fully inclusive means using a range of different approaches and resources to meet the needs of all individuals. It is very rare that a teacher or trainer has a group of learners who are all at the same level of ability, with the same prior knowledge and experience, and have the same needs. You don't have to individualise everything you do, you just need to take individual needs into account. Small group work and paired activities are a good way to use differentiation. You could group your learners for different activities by their learning preference, level of ability, level of qualification, past experiences or current knowledge. You are then ensuring all learners are included.

Being inclusive is also about establishing a purposeful learning environment where all your learners feel safe, secure, confident and valued. The venue, toilets and refreshment areas should be accessible and suitable for everyone; advance knowledge of your learners will help you check that everything is suitable. If your session includes a break, make sure you tell your learners what time this will be and for how long. If you don't, learners might not be concentrating on their learning but thinking about when they can go to the toilet or get a drink. You might be restricted by the availability of particular rooms or resources; therefore you need to be imaginative with what's available to you. Your learners don't need to know of any problems, as your professionalism should enable you to deliver and assess your subject effectively. However, you do need to take into account any health and safety issues and let your organisation know of any concerns.

If you are currently teaching, you could produce a case study regarding how you have created an inclusive teaching and learning environment with your learners.

You could cross-reference your response to the unit: Understanding and using inclusive teaching and learning approaches in education and training 1.1 if you have met the required criteria.

> 2.2 Explain why it is important to select teaching and learning approaches, resources and assessment methods to meet individual learner needs

Q24 In Chapter 4 (Q20) you compared the strengths and limitations of the teaching and learning approaches you could use for your subject, and stated how they could meet individual learner needs. Now list three resources, and three assessment methods, which you could use with your learners, and explain how they could meet individual learner needs.

You could cross-reference your response to the unit: Understanding and using inclusive teaching and learning approaches in education and training 1.2, whereby you explained how various teaching and learning approaches could meet individual learner needs. You therefore need only to address resources and assessment methods for this question.

Your response could explain that resources are all the aids, books, handouts, items of equipment, objects and people that you can use to deliver and assess your subject. They should stimulate learning, add impact and promote interest in the subject. Resources should be accessible and inclusive to all learners, while enabling them to acquire new skills, knowledge and understanding. When using or creating resources, ensure they promote equality of opportunity, reflect diversity and challenge stereotypes. Resources should be appropriate in terms of level, quality, quantity and content and be relevant to the subject and the learning expected. Handouts and presentations should be checked for spelling, grammar, punctuation and sentence construction as you don't want to give a bad example to your learners. You could create a table, which lists at least three resources and explains how they meet individual needs. For example:

Resource	Meeting individual needs
Handout to summarise a topic; hard copy and/or electronic	In a font, colour and style to suit a learner who has dyslexia. Rather than single a particular learner out, the same could be given to all learners. Electronic versions can be adapted by individual learners to suit their needs.
Physical resource such as a working model	To arouse the interest of a learner with a kinaesthetic learning preference. To encourage those with other learning preferences to try something out of their comfort zone.
Visiting speaker	To impart relevant information regarding a particular topic, which is pertinent to individual learners. To answer specific questions from learners which relate to their interest in the topic and their career aspirations.

You could explain that assessment is a way of finding out if learning has taken place. It enables you to ascertain if your learner has gained the required skills, knowledge, understanding and/or attitudes needed at a given point in time, towards their programme of learning.

It also provides your learners with an opportunity to demonstrate what progress they have made and to know what they have learnt so far. If you don't plan for and carry out any assessment with your learners, you will not know how well, or what, they have learnt. Assessment should not be in isolation from the teaching and learning process. You can assess that learning is taking place each time you are with your learners, for example, by asking questions or observing actions.

You could cross-reference your response to the unit: Understanding assessment in education and training 1.2 if you have met the required criteria.

You could then create a table, which lists at least three assessment methods and explains how they meet individual needs. For example:

Assessment method	Meeting individual needs
Discussion with a learner	Can support an observation in a restricted or confidential setting to check a learner's knowledge and understanding. Learners can describe how they carry out various activities that they might not be able to demonstrate to you because of limited access.
Gapped handout	To raise the morale of lower level learners by enabling them to fill in missing words from sentences. They can then feel a sense of achievement.
Project	Can help motivate a learner if their concentration lapses by encouraging them to choose their own relevant topic (with specific guidance from you). They can then take ownership of the project to work towards its completion.

Q25 Explain why it is important to select appropriate teaching and learning approaches, resources and assessment methods to meet individual needs.

Your response could explain that the teaching and learning approaches, resources and assessment methods you select will be based upon the requirements of the subject you will teach, and to meet the individual needs of your learners. If you don't select the right approaches, you might not deliver and assess in a way that effectively meets individual needs and ensures learning has taken place.

Other factors include the environment within which you will teach as this could affect the approaches you decide to use. This could be a classroom, workshop, training room or outdoor environment. You might also be influenced by which resources and equipment are available, and whether you teach individuals or groups. The time of day could have an impact, for example, you might wish to use an energiser activity after a lunch break in case your learners feel tired. The assessment methods you use should link to the required outcomes. You may need to devise informal methods to assess progress, and use formal methods to assess achievement. All the approaches and methods you use should be inclusive to your learners, and not exclude anyone for any reason.

If you are currently teaching, you could produce a case study regarding the teaching and learning approaches, resource and assessment methods you used with your learners, and how they met individual needs.

2.3 Explain ways to engage and motivate learners

Q26 What do the terms engaging and motivating mean?

Your response could state that engaging your learners is all about obtaining and maintaining their attention, involving them during the session and keeping them motivated. Motivation is the incentive or reason why someone chooses to do something. You need to be aware of how to engage your learners, and keep them motivated, as their keenness will affect their learning and behaviour during sessions.

Q27 Explain how you can engage and motivate your learners.

You could explain that to engage your learners from the beginning you would start by welcoming them to the session and stating the aims and objectives to capture their attention. To help settle your learners and focus their attention towards learning, you could use a starter activity. This could be a quiz to test knowledge gained so far, a discussion to open up thinking about the current topic, or an energiser activity focusing upon the session topic. Always include your learners by checking if they have any prior knowledge and/ or experience of the topic by asking them; you can then draw upon this during the session. Never assume your learners know or don't know something.

As you progress, allow time for questioning, repeating and summarising important points. Incorporate the knowledge and experience of your learners and, if you can, give relevant anecdotes to bring the subject to life. Ensure your session flows progressively, i.e. is delivered in a logical order and assesses progress before moving on to the next topic. When changing topics, try to link them together somehow or summarise one before moving on to the other. If particular learners finish earlier than others, you could give them an *extension activity* to stretch and challenge their learning further. It's always useful to carry a few spare activities around with you, or to have access to them electronically in case they are needed. When you summarise at the end of the session, don't introduce anything new as this might confuse your learners.

Using a variety of teaching and learning approaches will help meet all learning preferences and enable learning to take place. If you expect your learners to listen to you and then to remember everything you have said, as well as understand it, then very little learning will have taken place, unless it is their particular learning preference. If you can involve your learners with discussions, questions and activities with which they can engage, it will bring the subject to life and help learning to take place. Remember to use approaches, resources and assessment methods which focus on learners being *actively engaged* during the session and not just *passively listening* to you. It's not about *what you will teach*, but *how they will learn*. Approaches should always be fit for purpose, i.e. to enable learning to take place, and not just be used for the sake of it, or because you like to do things in a certain way.

Some learners may seem naturally enthusiastic and motivated about learning, but many need or expect you to inspire and engage them. You therefore need to promote a professional relationship that leads to individual trust and learning. Many factors affect a learner's motivation to work and to learn: for example, interest in the subject matter, perception of its usefulness, a general desire to achieve, self-confidence and self-esteem, as well as patience and persistence. Not all learners are motivated by the same values, needs, desires, or wants. Some of your learners will be motivated by the approval of others and some by overcoming personal challenges.

To help engage and motivate your learners you can:

- ask open questions (ones that begin with *who, what, when, where, why* and *how* – not closed questions, which just lead to *yes* or *no* responses)

- avoid creating intense competition, although some competition can be engaging and fun

- be aware of attention-span time limits

- give ongoing constructive feedback

- give praise and encouragement

- maintain an organised and orderly atmosphere

- make tasks interesting, practical and relevant

- negotiate realistic targets

- stretch and challenge learners' potential

- support those who need it

- treat learners with respect and as individuals

- use icebreakers and energisers to get learners actively working together

- vary your teaching and assessment approaches to reach all learning preferences

---

2.4 Summarise ways to establish ground rules with learners

Q28 What are ground rules and why use them?

Your response could state that ground rules are boundaries and rules to help create suitable conditions within which learners (and yourself) can safely work and learn. For example, switching off mobile devices and returning from breaks on time. They help to underpin appropriate behaviour and respect for others, and help the session flow more smoothly. If ground rules are not set, problems may occur which could disrupt the session and lead to misunderstandings or behaviour problems. This will then have an impact upon the learning taking place.

Depending upon the age of your learners, you could use the term *group contract* instead of ground rules. Ideally, the ground rules should be on display each time your group meets, and/or a typed version could be given to each learner, or uploaded to a virtual learning environment (VLE) or intranet if applicable. Even if you only have one or two learners, you should still agree some ground rules to help maintain behaviour and respect.

Q29 Summarise at least two ways in which you could establish ground rules with your learners.

Your response could state that it is best to agree the ground rules during the first meeting, perhaps after, or as part of an icebreaker once everyone is feeling more relaxed. Whenever possible, ground rules should be discussed and negotiated with your learners rather than forced upon them. Using an activity to do this will help learners feel included, take ownership of, and hopefully follow what was agreed. The types of ground rules you agree with your learners will depend upon their age and maturity.

You could then summarise how you would establish ground rules with your learners, for example, by asking what ground rules your learners would expect to follow as part of the programme. You need to have an idea of what will be non-negotiable, i.e. because of organisational requirements, i.e. health and safety, and what can be negotiable, i.e. break times. This way, you can steer the discussion to ensure all the non-negotiable ground rules are mentioned.

One way of establishing ground rules is where both you and your learners work together by a process of discussion and negotiation. This enables your learners to recognise what is and is not acceptable, giving them a sense of ownership and responsibility. It also enables learners to begin working together as a group and encourages aspects such as listening, compromise and respect for others.

Alternatively, your learners could write down the ground rules individually, then discuss in pairs and join into fours to create a poster or a list on flipchart paper. One or two learners could present this to the full group and agreement can then take place. You could then list the agreed ground rules for all to see.

Another way would be to ask your learners what others have done during previous events they have attended, which made learning difficult. They will usually come up with answers like mobile phones ringing or people interrupting others. You can then start creating a list by discussion and negotiation with the group.

Theory focus

References and further information

Appleyard, N and Appleyard, K (2010) *Communicating with Learners in the Lifelong Learning Sector.* Exeter: Learning Matters.

Belbin, M (1993, 1996, 2010) *Team Roles At Work.* Oxford: Elsevier Science & Technology.

Coffield, F (2008) *Just Suppose Teaching and Learning Became the First Priority.* London: Learning and Skills Network.

Dale, E (1969) *Audio Visual Methods in Teaching.* Texas: Holt Rinehart and Winston.

Dennick, R and Exley, K (2004) *Small Group Teaching: Tutorials, Seminars and Beyond.* Abingdon: Routledge.

Fleming, N (2005) *Teaching and Learning Preferences: VARK Strategies.* Honolulu: Honolulu Community College.

Gates, B – Creating great teachers video www.youtube.com/watch?v=1IcZbRY_bYs&feature=related

Gould, J (2012) *Learning Theory and Classroom Practice in the Lifelong Learning Sector* (2nd Edn). London: Learning Matters.

Gravells, A (2013) *The Award in Education and Training.* London: Learning Matters SAGE.

Kidd, W and Czerniawski ,G (2010) *Successful Teaching 14-19.* London: SAGE Publications Ltd.

Knowles, MS, Swanson, R and Elwood, F Holton III (2011) *The Adult Learner* (7th Edn). Oxford: Butterworth-Heinemann.

Laird, D (1985) *Approaches to Training and Development.* Harlow: Addison Wesley.

Learning preferences questionnaire – www.vark-learn.com

Lucas, B, Spencer, E and Claxton, G (2012) *How to Teach Vocational Education: A Theory of Vocational Pedagogy.* City & Guilds Centre for Skills Development, available at: www.skillsdevelopment.org/ PDF/How-to-teach-vocational-education.pdf

Maslow, AH (1987) (edited by Frager, R) *Motivation and Personality* (3rd Revised Edn). New York: Pearson Education Ltd.

Peart, S and Atkins, L (2011) *Teaching 14–19 Learners in the Lifelong Learning Sector.* Exeter: Learning Matters.

Rogers, A and Horrocks, N (2010) *Teaching Adults* (4th Edn). Maidenhead: Open University Press.

Vizard, D (2012) *How to Manage Behaviour in Further Education.* London: SAGE Publications Ltd.

Wallace, S (2007) *Getting the Buggers Motivated in FE* (2nd Edn). London: Continuum.

Wallace, S (2007) *Managing Behaviour in the Lifelong Learning Sector* (2nd Edn). Exeter: Learning Matters.

Websites

Behaviour tips – www.pivotaleducation.com

Belbin team roles – www.belbin.com

Dealing with behaviour – http://newteachers.tes.co.uk/content/dealing-behaviour-issues-%E2%80%93- guide-new-teachers

Icebreakers – http://adulted.about.com/od/icebreakerstp/toptenicebreakers.htm and http://www. mwls.co.uk/icebreakers/

Motivation – http://serc.carleton.edu/NAGTWorkshops/affective/motivation.html

Teaching and learning theories – http://classweb.gmu.edu/ndabbagh/Resources/IDKB/models_ theories.htm

Teaching groups – www.faculty.londondeanery.ac.uk/e-learning/small-group-teaching

Team roles – www.belbin.com

Tips for teaching adults – www.helium.com/knowledge/61278-tips-for-teaching-adult-learners- instead-of-younger-learners

Tuckman – www.infed.org/thinkers/tuckman.htm

UNIT TITLE: Understanding and using inclusive teaching and learning approaches in education and training
Assessment Grid

Learning outcomes The learner will:	Assessment criteria The learner can:	Example evidence
2. Understand ways to create an inclusive teaching and learning environment	2.1 Explain why it is important to create an inclusive teaching and learning environment	An explanation of why it is important to create an inclusive teaching and learning environment, for example, to ensure teaching and learning is successful for all. A case study of how you have created an inclusive teaching and learning environment for your learners (anonymised). *Cross-referenced to the unit: Understanding and using inclusive teaching and learning approaches in education and training 1.1.*
	2.2 Explain why it is important to select teaching and learning approaches, resources and assessment methods to meet individual learner needs	A list of teaching and learning approaches, such as: demonstrations; discussions; group work; projects; presentations; role plays; seminars. An explanation of how the approaches you have listed can meet the individual needs of learners. A list of resources you could use, such as: handouts; working models; visiting speakers. An explanation of how the resources you have listed can meet the needs of individual learners. A list of assessment methods you could use, such as: discussion; gapped handout; project. An explanation of how the assessment methods listed can meet the needs of individual learners. A case study regarding the teaching and learning approaches, resources and assessment methods you have used with your learners, and how they met their needs (anonymised). *Cross-referenced to the unit: Understanding and using inclusive teaching and learning approaches in education and training 1.2.* *Cross-referenced to the unit Understanding assessment in education and training 1.2.*

Learning outcomes The learner will:	Assessment criteria The learner can:	Example evidence
	2.3 Explain ways to engage and motivate learners	A definition of *engage* such as obtaining and maintaining attention, and involving all learners during the session. A definition of *motivate* such as the incentive or reason for doing something. An explanation of how you would engage and motivate learners during your sessions, for example, stating the aims and objectives and using a starter activity to capture attention.
	2.4 Summarise ways to establish ground rules with learners	A definition of ground rules, for example, rules and boundaries which should be followed by everyone, such as switching off mobile devices and returning from breaks on time. An explanation of why ground rules should be used with learners, for example, to help create suitable conditions within which learners (and yourself) can safely work and learn. A summary of ways to establish ground rules with learners, such as: discussions; paired activities, group activities.

6 BE ABLE TO PLAN INCLUSIVE TEACHING AND LEARNING

This chapter is in two parts. The first part, *Self assessment activities*, contains questions and activities which relate to the third learning outcome of the Award in Education and Training unit *Understanding and using inclusive teaching and learning approaches in education and training.*

The assessment criteria are shown in boxes and are followed by questions and activities for you to carry out. Ensure your responses are *specific to you*, the *subject* you will teach and the *context* and *environment* in which you will teach.

After completing the activities, check your responses with the second part: *Guidance for evidencing achievement.* This guidance is not intended to give you the answers to questions you may be asked in any formal assessments; however, it will help you focus your responses towards meeting the assessment criteria.

At the end of the chapter is an example of a completed *Assessment Grid,* which gives ideas for evidence you could provide towards meeting the assessment criteria. Evidence can be cross-referenced between units and assessment criteria if it meets the requirements.

Self assessment activities

3.1 Devise an inclusive teaching and learning plan

Q30 Devise and create an inclusive teaching and learning plan (often referred to as a session plan). This will be for your own learners if you are currently teaching, or for your peers (who will become your learners) as part of a micro-teach session. Your observer will advise you of the time length which might be 15 or 30 minutes.

3.2 Justify own selection of teaching and learning approaches, resources and assessment methods in relation to meeting individual learner needs

Q31 Justify how your selected teaching and learning approaches, resources and assessment methods will meet the individual needs of your learners.

Guidance for evidencing achievement

3.1 Devise an inclusive teaching and learning plan

Q30 Devise and create an inclusive teaching and learning plan (often referred to as a session plan). This will be for your own learners if you are currently teaching, or for your peers (who will become your learners) as part of a micro-teach session. Your observer will advise you of the time length which might be 15 or 30 minutes.

This is a practical activity for you to devise a plan of what you will deliver and assess for your micro-teach session. You should be given a pro-forma or template on which to create the content of your plan. If you are currently teaching, this should be the plan from your organisation. Your plan should be for the time length as stated by your observer. It should be inclusive, i.e. show how all learners will be involved and how you will meet any individual needs.

You could create a rationale first which is usually based on *who, what, when, where, why* and *how*. For example:

- group composition; number of learners and how their needs will be met through differentiation, equality and diversity and learning styles (who)

- subject and level (what)

- date, time and duration of the session (when)

- the venue (where)

- aim and objectives (why)

- the teaching and learning approaches, resources and assessment methods to be used, along with timings for each activity (how)

The rationale will help you focus upon the content of your plan, which should have a logical beginning, middle and end. It should take into account differentiation, equality and diversity, individual learning needs and learning preferences. You will need to ascertain these details in advance from your learners or peer group. You should clearly state your aim, i.e. what you want your learners to achieve during your session.

There should be a clear breakdown of the teaching and learning activities you plan to use. You will also need to consider what resources you will use, for example, an electronic presentation, flipchart paper, interactive whiteboard, pens, handouts, activities, text books, etc. The assessment activities should be stated so that you know how to assess that learning has taken place, for example, questions, observation, etc.

Timings should be listed, for example, 2.00 p.m., 2.05 p.m., etc. next to each activity, alternatively you could state 5 minutes, 7 minutes, etc. for each activity.

Your plan should be realistic, don't attempt to achieve too much from either yourself or your learners. Consider an activity you could remove if you run out of time, and something extra you could add in if you have spare time. It is also useful to have some spare activities for learners who may finish earlier than others, and extension activities for learners who are more able and/or like further challenges. You should have a contingency plan in case anything goes wrong, such as a hard copy of a computerised presentation. Always end your session plan with a summary linking back to your aim and the objectives, and allow time for learner questions.

Please see Chapter 13 for further information regarding the micro-teach session, and an example plan.

> 3.2 Justify own selection of teaching and learning approaches, resources and assessment methods in relation to meeting individual learner needs

Q31 Justify how your selected teaching and learning approaches, resources and assessment methods will meet the individual needs of your learners.

Your response should justify how you plan to meet the individual needs of your learners through the teaching and learning approaches, resources and assessment methods you plan to use. It would be useful if you can obtain details of your learners or peer group in advance to ascertain their learning preferences and/or any individual needs.

You might have learners of different abilities and/or levels within the same group, therefore you will need to state how the different teaching and learning activities will be used to stretch and challenge your learners. You could plan to use varied activities and incorporate individual, paired or group work. If your group contains mainly kinaesthetic learners, planning practical activities will help them learn best. However, make sure you use strategies which cover all learning preferences to ensure all learners in the group can benefit.

Your resources should not create any barriers to learning, should be accessible to all and meet any individual needs. For example, you might have a learner who has dyslexia who may benefit from a pastel coloured background for presentations or handouts. All learners can benefit from this rather than singling out and possibly embarrassing one person.

The assessment methods you choose should relate to the topic you are delivering. If you have learners of different abilities and/or levels, you could use differentiated activities to meet these needs. For example, a gapped handout, a crossword or a multiple choice test which are all based on the same topic. You will need to plan whether you are assessing progress and/or achievement. If you are assessing progress, the methods you use might be informal, such as a discussion or oral questions. Formal methods could include written questions to assess knowledge and understanding, and observation to assess skills. If you are assessing group activities, make sure you know the contributions of each individual.

Theory focus

References and further information

Avis, J, Fisher, R and Thompson, R (2011) *Teaching in Lifelong Learning: A Guide To Theory And Practice.* Oxford: Oxford University Press.

Fleming, N (2005) *Teaching and Learning Styles: VARK Strategies*. Honolulu: Honolulu Community College.

Gravells, A (2013) *The Award in Education and Training* (5th Edn). London: Learning Matters SAGE.

Gravells, A and Simpson, S (2012) *Equality and Diversity in the Lifelong Learning Sector* (2nd Edn). London: Learning Matters.

Reece, I and Walker, S (2007) *Teaching, Training and Learning: A Practical Guide* (6th Edn). Tyne & Wear: Business Education Publishers.

Wallace, S (2011) *Teaching, Tutoring and Training in the Lifelong Learning Sector* (4th Edn). Exeter: Learning Matters.

Websites

Assessment methods – www.brookes.ac.uk/services/ocsld/resources/methods.html

Fleming's Learning Styles – www.vark-learn.com

UNIT TITLE: Understanding and using inclusive teaching and learning approaches in education and training
Assessment Grid

Learning outcomes The learner will:	Assessment criteria The learner can:	Example evidence
3. Be able to plan inclusive teaching and learning	3.1 Devise an inclusive teaching and learning plan	A rationale for your micro-teach session based on who, what, when, where, why and how. A teaching and learning plan: this is a pro-forma or template which you should complete. The plan should be inclusive, and have a clear aim of what you want your learners to achieve, with objectives stating how they will achieve them.
	3.2 Justify own selection of teaching and learning approaches, resources and assessment methods in relation to meeting individual learner needs	A justification of the reasons why you have selected your teaching and learning approaches in relation to meeting individual learner needs. For example, to meet the different abilities and/ or levels of learners in the group. A justification of the resources you will use in relation to meeting individual learner needs. For example, providing handouts on pastel coloured paper to all learners, not just for the learner who has dyslexia. A justification of the assessment methods you will use in relation to meeting individual learner needs. For example, differentiation in the form of a gapped handout, a crossword or a multiple-choice test all based on the same topic.

7 BE ABLE TO DELIVER INCLUSIVE TEACHING AND LEARNING

This chapter is in two parts. The first part, *Self assessment activities*, contains questions and activities which relate to the fourth learning outcome of the Award in Education and Training unit *Understanding and using inclusive teaching and learning approaches in education and training.*

The assessment criteria are shown in boxes and are followed by questions and activities for you to carry out. Ensure your responses are *specific to you*, the *subject* you will teach and the *context* and *environment* in which you will teach.

After completing the activities, check your responses with the second part: *Guidance for evidencing achievement*. This guidance is not intended to give you the answers to questions you may be asked in any formal assessments; however, it will help you focus your responses towards meeting the assessment criteria.

At the end of the chapter is an example of a completed *Assessment Grid,* which gives ideas for evidence you could provide towards meeting the assessment criteria. Evidence can be cross-referenced between units and assessment criteria if it meets the requirements.

Self assessment activities

> 4.1 Use teaching and learning approaches, resources and assessment methods to meet individual learner needs

Q32 Deliver your planned session to your learners. During the delivery, ensure you use a range of appropriate teaching and learning approaches, resources and assessment methods to meet the individual needs of your learners.

> 4.2 Communicate with learners in ways that meet their individual needs

Q33 During the delivery of your session, ensure you effectively communicate with your learners in ways that meet their individual needs.

> 4.3 Provide constructive feedback to learners to meet their individual needs

Q34 During the delivery of your session, provide constructive feedback to your learners to meet their individual needs. This should relate to their progress and achievement towards your planned aim.

Guidance for evidencing achievement

> 4.1 Use teaching and learning approaches, resources and assessment methods to meet individual learner needs

Q32 Deliver your planned session to your learners. During the delivery, ensure you use a range of appropriate teaching and learning approaches, resources and assessment methods to meet the individual needs of your learners.

This is a practical task which enables you to deliver a session to your peers (or perhaps to your current learners if you are an in-service teacher or trainer). When delivering your session, make sure you demonstrate confidence, and convey passion and enthusiasm for your subject. Through the teaching and learning approaches you use, you need to actively engage your learners and meet any individual needs.

The resources you use should support inclusive learning and teaching and could include electronic presentation equipment, interactive white boards, flipchart paper and pens, specialist equipment, projectors, digital media, books and handouts, etc. All resources should be checked in advance to ensure they are inclusive, fit for purpose, safe and fully operational. If you are delivering a session to your peers, you will need to arrive early to check the room you will be using. You may need to ask your observer in advance what materials and equipment are available for you to use. If you are planning to use an electronic presentation it would be useful to e-mail this to your observer in advance for them to check it, in case the version you plan to use isn't compatible. All resources you use should be relevant to the subject you are teaching and the individual needs of your learners.

To ensure learning has taken place you need to use appropriate assessment methods, for example, asking questions or observing practice.

You will be observed delivering your session and you should receive verbal and written feedback afterwards from your observer and possibly from your peers. You might be asked to give your observer a copy of your plan in advance. This will enable them to ask any questions regarding your choice of teaching and learning approaches and how you plan to engage and assess your learners. Your observer will be able to give you feedback regarding the structure of your plan to achieve your aim, and the objectives you plan to use. You might also be visually recorded to enable you to view your session afterwards to aid the self-evaluation process.

You could provide your plan, your observer's feedback form, any peer feedback forms received, and examples of activities and resources you have used as evidence to meet the assessment criteria.

Please see Chapter 13 for further information regarding the micro-teach session.

4.2 Communicate with learners in ways that meet their individual needs

Q33 During the delivery of your session, ensure you effectively communicate with your learners in ways that meet their individual needs.

This is a practical task which enables you to communicate and interact with your learners. You should use methods which engage and motivate your learners, and meet their individual needs.

The person observing your session will want to see you demonstrate appropriate communication techniques. You might find it helpful to ask them for a copy of their observation form beforehand, to see what they will be looking for.

Your observer will be watching how you introduce your session, how you enable your learners to feel at ease and participate, and how you facilitate the teaching, learning and assessment activities. They will want to see that you are confident and professional and that you deal with any situations as they arise. To help meet individual needs, you may need to adapt the activities you are using. You should be aware of your body language, any regional dialects or accents, and the amount of jargon, technical terms or acronyms you use.

Successful communication includes:

- oral communication, i.e. the way you speak when explaining, describing, summarising, questioning and giving feedback – be aware of your voice projection and when to use pauses to gain attention or allow thinking time

- written communication, i.e. presentations, handouts, worksheets, written feedback and progress reports – always check your spelling, grammar, punctuation and sentence construction

- non-verbal communication, i.e. the way you act, your body language, appearance, facial expressions, eye contact, gestures, posture and non-verbal signals

- questioning, i.e. oral or written should include all learners and preferably use open questions

- listening skills, i.e. eye contact, not interrupting, not being judgemental

- other qualities you can convey such as empathy (compassion and understanding for a learner's situation), and sympathy (consideration for what a learner has experienced)

The language you use should reflect equality and inclusiveness, be relevant to the subject, not offend anyone in any way and be at the right level. You may have to practise with your voice projection, but don't shout, just speak a little louder and slower than normal and ask if all learners can hear you. Sometimes nerves might make you speak faster.

Don't expect your learners to remember everything first time; they don't know what you know. You should repeat or rephrase key points regularly. Try not to get frustrated if asked questions regarding points you have already explained, and don't say things like *I just told you that* or *Can't you remember what I just said?* Instead, rephrase what you have said, or ask another learner to attempt an explanation. Repeating key points will help your learners remember them. Don't embarrass a learner in front of their peer group; they may feel they can't ask you anything again. Learning occurs best in an active, not a passive, environment where communication is a two-way process.

You could provide your plan, your observer's feedback form, any peer feedback forms received, and examples of activities and resources you have used as evidence to meet the assessment criteria.

4.3 Provide constructive feedback to learners to meet their individual needs

Q34 During the delivery of your session, provide constructive feedback to your learners to meet their individual needs. This should relate to their progress and achievement towards your planned aim.

This is a practical task enabling you to demonstrate how you provide constructive feedback to your learners.

The person observing your session will want to see you demonstrate how you provide constructive feedback to meet the individual needs of your learners. For example, if a learner is struggling to answer a question, you could rephrase it if you don't get the response you expect.

During your micro-teach session, you should give constructive feedback to each individual learner after an assessment activity. Feedback should confirm progress, achievement or otherwise, be given in a manner that will help your learner, and be constructive and developmental. Good feedback should offer guidance and information towards the subject aim; as it is not a judgement of personality or character.

Please see Chapter 11 for more information regarding giving constructive feedback.

You could provide your plan, your observer's feedback form, any peer feedback forms received, and examples of activities and resources you have used as evidence to meet the assessment criteria.

Theory focus

References and further information

Appleyard, N and Appleyard, K (2010) *Communicating with Learners in the Lifelong Learning Sector.* Exeter: Learning Matters.

Gravells, A (2013) *The Award in Education and Training.* London: Learning Matters SAGE.

Guilds Centre for Skills Development, available at: www.skillsdevelopment.org/PDF/How-to-teach-vocational-education.pdf

Hill, C (2008) *Teaching with e-learning in the Lifelong Learning Sector* (2nd Edn). Exeter: Learning Matters.

Knowles, MS, Swanson, R and Elwood, F Holton III (2005) *The Adult Learner: The Definitive Classic in Adult Education and Human Resource Development*. Oxford: Butterworth-Heinemann.

Lucas, B, Spencer, E and Claxton, G (2012) *How to Teach Vocational Education: A Theory of Vocational Pedagogy*. City & Guilds.

Read, H (2011) *The Best Assessor's Guide*. Bideford: Read On Publications Ltd.

Reece, I and Walker, S (2007) *Teaching, Training and Learning: A Practical Guide* (6th Edn). Tyne & Wear: Business Education Publishers.

Tummons, T (2011) *Assessing Learning in the Lifelong Learning Sector*. Exeter: Learning Matters.

Wallace, S (2011) *Teaching, Tutoring and Training in the Lifelong Learning Sector* (4th Edn). Exeter: Learning Matters.

Websites

Assessment tools (literacy, numeracy, ESOL, dyslexia) – www.excellencegateway.org.uk/toolslibrary

Developing Assessment Feedback – http://escalate.ac.uk/4147

Feedback – http://escalate.ac.uk/4147

Theories of learning and teaching – www.learningandteaching.info/learning/

**UNIT TITLE: Understanding and using inclusive teaching
and learning approaches in education and training
Assessment Grid**

Learning outcomes The learner will:	Assessment criteria The learner can:	Example evidence
4. Be able to deliver inclusive teaching and learning	4.1 Use teaching and learning approaches, resources and assessment methods to meet individual learner needs	Teaching and learning plan. Completed observer's feedback form. Completed peer feedback forms (received from others – if applicable). Copies of teaching and learning activities used such as notes and worksheets. Copies of resources used such as handouts and presentations. Copies of assessment activities used such as written questions. Copy of a visual recording of the session (if used).
	4.2 Communicate with learners in ways that meet their individual needs	Completed observer's feedback form. Completed peer feedback forms (received from others – if applicable). Copy of a visual recording of the session (if used).
	4.3 Provide constructive feedback to learners to meet their individual needs	Completed observer's feedback form. Completed peer feedback forms (received from others – if applicable). Copy of a visual recording of the session (if used).

8 BE ABLE TO EVALUATE THE DELIVERY OF INCLUSIVE TEACHING AND LEARNING

This chapter is in two parts. The first part, *Self assessment activities*, contains questions and activities which relate to the fifth learning outcome of the Award in Education and Training unit *Understanding and using inclusive teaching and learning approaches in education and training.*

The assessment criteria are shown in boxes and are followed by questions and activities for you to carry out. Ensure your responses are *specific to you*, the *subject* you will teach and the *context* and *environment* in which you will teach.

After completing the activities, check your responses with the second part: *Guidance for evidencing achievement*. This guidance is not intended to give you the answers to questions you may be asked in any formal assessments; however, it will help you focus your responses towards meeting the assessment criteria.

At the end of the chapter is an example of a completed **Assessment Grid,** which gives ideas for evidence you could provide towards meeting the assessment criteria. Evidence can be cross-referenced between units and assessment criteria if it meets the requirements.

Self assessment activities

5.1 Review the effectiveness of own delivery of inclusive teaching and learning

Q35 After you have delivered your micro-teach session, review the effectiveness of the teaching and learning approaches you used.

5.2 Identify areas for improvement in own delivery of inclusive teaching and learning

Q36 Based on the feedback from your observer and peers (if applicable), and your own considerations of how you delivered your session, identify areas for improvement.

Guidance for evidencing achievement

5.1 Review the effectiveness of own delivery of inclusive teaching and learning

Q35 After you have delivered your micro-teach session, review the effectiveness of the teaching and learning approaches you used.

Your response should review the different inclusive teaching and learning approaches you used and how effective they were. You could give specific examples, for example, you might have felt that using a discussion was lively and generated a good debate; however, not every learner contributed. Next time, you would ensure you involved each learner in some way, perhaps by asking individual questions.

Reviewing your session includes thinking about what you have done and how you could improve or modify it for the future. You might think everything has gone well; if this is the case, consider *why* it went well to see if you could use the techniques again. Evaluating the effectiveness of your own teaching includes making a decision as to how successful the session was and how successful you were at facilitating learning. For example, you might state that you felt the session was a success as your learners were able to answer all the questions you asked, or demonstrate a skill. However, if not all learners were given the opportunity to answer a question or to demonstrate a skill, you won't know what they have learnt.

You might have been given a *self-evaluation form* to complete after your session, or you might be maintaining an ongoing *reflective learning journal*. Before completing these, consider what went well, what didn't and why. As well as your own perceptions of your session, you need to take into account the feedback you have received from your observer and your peers (if applicable), before making a decision. If your session was visually recorded, watch it to help you see how you appear to others, for example, how you speak or react to different situations. You might be surprised to see things you didn't know you did.

You could provide your observer's feedback form, peer feedback forms received (if applicable), a completed self-evaluation form or reflective learning journals as evidence to meet the assessment criteria.

5.2 Identify areas for improvement in own delivery of inclusive teaching and learning

Q36 Based on the feedback from your observer and peers (if applicable), and your own considerations of how you delivered your session, identify areas for improvement.

Your response should identify the areas you feel you could improve upon regarding your delivery of inclusive teaching and learning.

For example:

- check handouts for spelling errors as you had made a mistake

- don't give a handout part way through unless it is really relevant, as it disrupted the group

- have an extra activity for learners as some finished a task earlier than others

- keep jargon to a minimum when the topic is new so as not to confuse anyone

- plan ahead to get enough copies of the presentation for everyone as you were one short

- remember to ask if anyone has any knowledge or experience of the subject at the beginning of the session: this could then be drawn upon during the session

- try not to say 'erm', 'yeah' and 'okay' so much as it could be off putting

- use differentiated activities to stretch and challenge learners of all levels

- use more eye contact with learners to make them feel included

- use paired activities and peer assessment to help the learners check their own progress

Alternatively, you could identify your strengths and limitations. For example:

Strengths:

- being prepared and setting up the area/checking all equipment in advance

- clearing up afterwards

- displaying positive body language

- introducing and summarising the aim and objectives

- using a variety of teaching and learning activities

Limitations:

- didn't ask every learner an open question to check knowledge

- didn't manage to keep to the session plan timings, which resulted in time to spare at the end

- gave a handout too early which meant learners were reading ahead rather than focusing on the point being discussed

Based on your response to the question, and any strengths and limitations you have identified, you could create an *action plan* for your own improvement and development. For example, you might wish to attend an English session to help improve your spelling. You could provide evidence of continuing professional development (CPD) as proof you have done something regarding the areas you have identified for improvement.

Theory focus

References and further information

Brookfield, SD (1995) *Becoming a Critically Reflective Teacher*. San Francisco, CA: Jossey-Bass.

Gravells, A (2013) *The Award in Education and Training*. London: Learning Matters SAGE.

Reece, I and Walker, S (2007) *Teaching, Training and Learning; A Practical Guide* (6th Edn). Tyne & Wear: Business Education Publishers Ltd.

Roffey-Barentsen, J and Malthouse, R (2012) *Reflective Practice in Education and Training* (2nd Edn). Exeter: Learning Matters.

Schön, D (1983) *The Reflective Practitioner*. San Francisco, CA: Jossey-Bass.

Wallace, S (2011) *Teaching, Tutoring and Training in the Lifelong Learning Sector* (4th Edn). Exeter: Learning Matters.

Websites

Reflective practice – www.learningandteaching.info/learning/reflecti.htm

UNIT TITLE: Understanding and using inclusive teaching and learning approaches in education and training
Assessment Grid

Learning outcomes The learner will:	Assessment criteria The learner can:	Example evidence
5. Be able to evaluate the delivery of inclusive teaching and learning	5.1 Review the effectiveness of own delivery of inclusive teaching and learning	A review of the different delivery approaches you used during your session and how effective they were. Completed observer's feedback form. Completed peer feedback forms (received from others – if applicable). Completed self-evaluation form. Reflective learning journals.
	5.2 Identify areas for improvement in own delivery of inclusive teaching and learning	An identification of areas for improvement regarding your delivery. A list of your own strengths and limitations. An action plan for your own development. Evidence of continuing professional development (CPD).

9 UNDERSTAND TYPES AND METHODS OF ASSESSMENT USED IN EDUCATION AND TRAINING

This chapter is in two parts. The first part, *Self assessment activities*, contains questions and activities which relate to the first learning outcome of the Award in Education and Training unit *Understanding assessment in education and training.*

The assessment criteria are shown in boxes and are followed by questions and activities for you to carry out. Ensure your responses are *specific to you*, the *subject* you will teach and the *context* and *environment* in which you will teach.

After completing the activities, check your responses with the second part: *Guidance for evidencing achievement*. This guidance is not intended to give you the answers to questions you may be asked in any formal assessments; however, it will help you focus your responses towards meeting the assessment criteria.

At the end of the chapter is an example of a completed *Assessment Grid,* which gives ideas for evidence you could provide towards meeting the assessment criteria. Evidence can be cross-referenced between units and assessment criteria if it meets the requirements.

Self assessment activities

1.1 Explain the purpose of types of assessment used in education and training

Q37 List at least three examples of types of assessment.

Q38 Explain the purpose of (i.e. the reasons for) the types of assessment you have listed in Q37.

1.2 Describe characteristics of different methods of assessment in education and training

Q39 List at least six different methods of assessment which you could use with your learners.

Q40 Describe the characteristics (i.e. uniqueness) of the assessment methods you have listed in Q39.

1.3 Compare the strengths and limitations of different assessment methods in relation to meeting individual learner needs

Q41 Compare the strengths and limitations of the six different assessment methods you have listed in Q39, and explain how they could meet individual learner needs.

1.4 Explain how different assessment methods can be adapted to meet individual learner needs

Q42 List at least three assessment methods and explain how they could be adapted to meet individual learner needs.

Guidance for evidencing achievement

1.1 Explain the purpose of types of assessment used in education and training

Q37 List at least three examples of types of assessment.

Your list could include some of the following:

- initial

- diagnostic

- formative

- summative

- holistic

Q38 Explain the purpose of (i.e. the reasons for) the types of assessment you have listed in Q37.

Your response could state that assessment types relate to the purpose of assessment, i.e. the reason assessment is carried out. Assessment is a way of finding out if learning has taken place. It enables you to ascertain if your learner has gained the required skills, knowledge, understanding and/or attitudes needed at a given point in time, towards their programme of learning. It also provides your learners with an opportunity to demonstrate what progress they have made and what they have learnt. If you don't plan for and carry out any assessment with your learners, you will not know how well, or what, they have learnt. Assessment should not be in isolation from the teaching and learning process.

Depending upon the subject you are assessing and any relevant qualification requirements, you might carry out various types of assessment with your learners which could be on a formal or informal basis. Formal assessment means the results will count towards achievement of something, for example, a qualification. Informal assessments help you see how your learners are progressing at a given point.

You might have listed initial, formative and summative types of assessment for your response to question 37. You could then explain their purpose.

Initial assessment – this will give you information regarding your learners, for example, any specific learning and assessment requirements or needs they may have, or any further training and support they may require. The process will also ensure learners are on the right programme. This should take place prior to, or when learners commence. Initial assessment should ascertain a learner's previous skills, knowledge and understanding. A quick question, *What experience do you have of this, if any?* will soon give you some idea of what your learner already knows.

Formative assessment – this should take place continually throughout your learners' time with you. This type of assessment is usually carried out informally to review progress, identify any support requirements, and inform further development. Simply asking questions and observing actions can help you assess how your learners are progressing. Assessing your learners on a formative basis will enable you to see if they are ready for a summative or final assessment. You could use activities, quizzes and short tasks for learners to carry out which would make the assessment process more interesting, and highlight any areas which need further development. Formative assessment is usually informal, devised by yourself, and often called assessment *for* learning as it will help prepare learners for formal assessment.

Summative assessment – this usually occurs at the end of a session, programme, topic, unit or full qualification. Summative assessment is a measure of achievement towards set requirements or criteria rather than focusing on progress. This type of assessment can often be quite stressful to learners, and sometimes lead to a fail result even though the learner is quite capable under other circumstances. If you are assessing a programme where the activities are provided for you, for example, examinations or tests, there is often a tendency to teach purely what is required to achieve a pass. Teaching to pass examinations or tests does not maximise a learner's ability and potential. They might be able to answer the questions just by relying on their memory. This doesn't help them in life and work, as they might not be able to put theory into practice afterwards, or even understand the knowledge they have gained. Knowing something, and understanding it, are quite different. Summative assessment is usually formal, devised by the awarding organisa- tion who accredits the qualification, and often called assessment *of* learning as it counts towards the achievement of something.

> 1.2 Describe characteristics of different methods of assessment in education and training

Q39 List at least six different methods of assessment which you could use with your learners.

Your list could include some of the following:

- assignments
- case studies
- discussions
- essays
- examinations
- gapped handouts
- journals/diaries
- multiple-choice questions
- observations
- peer and self assessment
- projects
- puzzles and crosswords
- questions: oral or written
- tests

Q40 Describe the characteristics (i.e. uniqueness) of the assessment methods you have listed in Q39.

Your response could state that assessment methods should be suited to the level and ability of your learners, and whether they are informal, to assess progress, or formal, to assess achievement. The characteristics of the assessment methods chosen will very much depend upon the subject you are assessing, and the context and environment you are assessing in.

You could describe the characteristics of the six assessment methods you have listed in your response to question 39.

For example, the characteristics of the first six from the previous bullet list:

Assignments – these can be practical or theoretical tasks to assess various aspects of a subject or qualification over a short or long period of time.

Case studies – these could be based on a hypothetical situation, a description of an actual event or an incomplete event, enabling learners to explore and analyse the situation and give suggestions.

Discussions – these enable learners to talk about a relevant topic either individually with the assessor, in groups or pairs. The term *professional discussion* is sometimes used as the discussion is usually based upon the assessment criteria of a qualification.

Essays – these are formal pieces of written text, produced by a learner, for a specific topic. There are often other requirements to meet such as the use of academic writing, referencing quotes and meeting word count limits.

Examinations – these are a formal activity which must be carried out in certain conditions, for example in a controlled environment and within a given time limit.

Gapped handouts – these are interactive handouts to check knowledge (they can also be electronic) which have sentences with words missing which learners complete.

If you are currently teaching, you could include examples of actual assessment activities you have used with your learners.

You could cross-reference your response to the unit: Understanding and using inclusive teaching and learning approaches in education and training 2.2 if you have met the required criteria.

> 1.3 Compare the strengths and limitations of different assessment methods in relation to meeting individual learner needs

Q41 Compare the strengths and limitations of the six different assessment methods you have listed in Q39, and explain how they could meet individual learner needs.

You could create a table to compare the assessment methods you have identified, and explain how they could meet individual learner needs; for example, for the first six assessment methods from the previous bullet list.

Assessment method	Strengths	Limitations	Meeting individual needs
Assignments	Consolidates learning. Several aspects of a qualification can be assessed. Some assignments are set by the awarding organisation who will give clear marking criteria.	Everything must have been taught beforehand or be known by the learner. Questions can be misinterpreted. Can be time consuming for learners to complete. Must be individually assessed and written feedback given. Assessor might be biased when marking.	Ideal for learners who like to progress at their own pace. Learners might be able to add to their work if they don't meet all the requirements first time.
Case studies	Can make topics more realistic. Can be carried out individually or in a group situation.	If carried out as a group activity, roles should be defined and individual contributions assessed. Time should be allowed for a de-brief. Must have clear outcomes. Can be time consuming to prepare and assess.	They can enhance motivation and interest. Build on the current knowledge and experience of individual learners.
Discussions	All learners can be encouraged to participate. Allows freedom of view points, questions and discussions. Can contribute to meeting assessment criteria. Ideal way to assess aspects which are more difficult to observe, are rare occurrences, or take place in restricted or confidential settings. Useful to support observations to check knowledge. Learners can describe how they carry out various activities.	Easy to digress. Assessor needs to keep the group focused and set a time limit. Some learners may not get involved, therefore quieter learners won't be fully assessed. Some learners may dominate. The assessor needs to manage the contributions of all individuals. Can be time consuming. Learners may need to research a topic in advance. Can lead to arguments. Thorough records need to be kept of what was achieved and by whom.	A learner with a visual impairment could discuss responses rather than writing or using a computer to questions.

(Continued)

(Continued)

Assessment method	Strengths	Limitations	Meeting individual needs
Essays	Useful for academic subjects. Can check a learner's English skills at specific levels. Enhances a learner's knowledge by using research and reading.	Not suitable for lower level learners. Marking can be time consuming. Plagiarism can be an issue. Doesn't usually have a right or wrong answer therefore difficult to grade. Learners need good writing skills.	A learner with dyslexia could complete it using a word processor with a spell check facility.
Examinations	Can be *open book*, or *open notes*, enabling learners to have books and notes with them.	Invigilation required. Security arrangements to be in place prior to, and afterwards for examination papers. Learners may have been taught purely to pass expected questions by using past papers, therefore they may forget everything afterwards. Some learners may be anxious. Can be *closed book*, or *closed notes*, not allowing learners to have books and notes with them. Results might take a while to be processed. If a learner fails, they may have to wait a period of time before a re-take.	Ideal for learners who like the challenge of a formal examination and cope well under the circumstances
Gapped handouts	Informal assessment activity which can be done individually, in pairs or groups.	Mature learners may consider them inappropriate. Too many worksheets can be boring. Learners might not be challenged enough.	Ideal for lower level learners. Can be created at different degrees of difficulty to address differentiation.

> 1.4 Explain how different assessment methods can be adapted to meet individual learner needs

Q42 List at least three assessment methods and explain how they could be adapted to meet individual learner needs.

Your response could list three assessment methods from your response to question 39 and explain how they could be adapted to meet individual needs, such as multiple-choice questions, projects and tests.

Multiple-choice questions – providing the information in an alternative format such as spoken instead of written. This would suit a learner who has impaired vision and can't read very well, or a learner who has dyslexia and might confuse the letters b and d.

Projects – incorporating new and emerging technologies to help improve the confidence of a learner who is not used to using a computer.

Tests – translating into another language, or bilingually for learners whose first language is not English. Using larger print or Braille for learners with a visual impairment.

Your response should include the fact that you would need to check with your organisation regarding what you can and can't do, as you may need approval to make any adaptations or reasonable adjustments.

If you are currently teaching, you could produce a case study of how you have adapted different assessment methods to meet individual learners' needs.

Theory focus

References and further information

Gravells, A (2013) *The Award in Education and Training*. London: Learning Matters SAGE.

Gravells, A (2012) *Achieving your TAQA Assessor and Internal Quality Assurer Award*. London: Learning Matters.

Read, H (2011) *The Best Assessor's Guide*. Bideford: Read On Publications Ltd.

Read, H (2013) *The Best Initial Assessment Guide*. Bideford: Read On Publications Ltd.

Tummons, T (2011) *Assessing Learning in the Lifelong Learning Sector*. Exeter: Learning Matters.

Wilson, L A (2012) *Practical Teaching: A Guide to Assessment and Quality Assurance*. Andover: Cengage Learning

Websites

Assessment tools (literacy, numeracy, ESOL, dyslexia) – www.excellencegateway.org.uk/toolslibrary

Developing Assessment Feedback – http://escalate.ac.uk/4147

Plagiarism – www.plagiarism.org and www.plagiarismadvice.org

UNIT TITLE: Understanding assessment in education and training
Assessment Grid

Learning outcomes The learner will:	Assessment criteria The learner can:	Example evidence
1. Understand types and methods of assessment used in education and training	1.1 Explain the purpose of types of assessment used in education and training	A list of at least three types of assessment, for example, initial, formative and summative. An explanation of the purpose of each of the types of assessment you have listed. For example, the reasons why initial, formative and summative types of assessment are used with learners.
	1.2 Describe characteristics of different methods of assessment in education and training	A list of at least six different methods of assessment, such as: assignments; case studies; discussions; essays; examinations; gapped handouts. A description of the characteristics of each of the methods of assessment you have listed, for example, assignments: these can be practical or theoretical tasks to assess various aspects of a subject or qualification over a short or long period of time. Examples of actual assessment activities used with learners. *Cross-referenced to the unit Understanding and using inclusive teaching and learning approaches in education and training 2.2.*
	1.3 Compare the strengths and limitations of different assessment methods in relation to meeting individual learner needs	A comparison of the strengths and limitations of at least six different assessment methods. This could be displayed in a table with the headings: assessment method, strengths, limitations, meeting individual needs. An explanation of how the assessment methods can meet individual learner needs, for example, assignments are ideal for learners who like to progress at their own pace. Learners might be able to add to their work if they don't meet all the requirements first time.
	1.4 Explain how different assessment methods can be adapted to meet individual learner needs	An explanation of how at least three different assessment methods can be adapted to meet individual learner needs. For example, tests: translating into another language. A case study relating to how you have adapted different assessment methods to meet individual learner needs (anonymised).

10 UNDERSTAND HOW TO INVOLVE LEARNERS AND OTHERS IN THE ASSESSMENT PROCESS

This chapter is in two parts. The first part, **Self assessment activities**, contains questions and activities which relate to the second learning outcome of the Award in Education and Training unit **Understanding assessment in education and training.**

The assessment criteria are shown in boxes and are followed by questions and activities for you to carry out. Ensure your responses are *specific to you*, the *subject* you will teach and the *context* and *environment* in which you will teach.

After completing the activities, check your responses with the second part: **Guidance for evidencing achievement**. This guidance is not intended to give you the answers to questions you may be asked in any formal assessments; however, it will help you focus your responses towards meeting the assessment criteria.

At the end of the chapter is an example of a completed **Assessment Grid,** which gives ideas for evidence you could provide towards meeting the assessment criteria. Evidence can be cross-referenced between units and assessment criteria if it meets the requirements.

Self assessment activities

> 2.1 Explain why it is important to involve learners and others in the assessment process

Q43 Explain why it is important to involve learners in the assessment process.

Q44 Explain why it is important to involve others in the assessment process.

> 2.2 Explain the role and use of peer- and self-assessment in the assessment process

Q45 What is the role of peer- and self-assessment?

Q46 Explain how peer- and self-assessment can be used with learners in the assessment process.

> 2.3 Identify sources of information that should be made available to learners and others involved in the assessment process

Q47 List at least four sources of information which will prove beneficial to learners and others who are involved in the assessment process.

Q48 Identify where the sources of information can be located.

Guidance for evidencing achievement

2.1 Explain why it is important to involve learners and others in the assessment process

Q43 Explain why it is important to involve learners in the assessment process.

Your response could explain that it's important to involve learners in the assessment process from commencement to completion to ensure they are fully briefed and involved. For example, initial assessment involves the learner in discussions so that the results can be used as a foundation on which to agree a suitable individual learning plan (ILP), action, or assessment plan. Assessment planning documents form the basis of what will be learnt and assessed, they usually follow an outline of who, what, when, where, why and how. This information will also help you plan an appropriate course of action should any support be necessary. Involving your learners gives them the opportunity to inform you of anything which might affect their progress and/or achievement. It also helps them take ownership of their progress and development if they have a copy of what is to be assessed.

It might be that one of your learners has already achieved a unit or part of the programme requirements elsewhere. You could ascertain if they have any evidence of this, i.e. proof of their achievement, to enable you to instigate the process of recognition of prior learning (RPL). If your learner wasn't involved at this stage, they could unnecessarily repeat certain aspects.

If you are teaching or training as well as assessing, you can involve your learners at the commencement of a session by asking them what they already know. In this way, you can draw and build upon their experiences throughout the session. At the end of the session you could involve your learners by asking them what they feel they have learnt, and how they can apply it to other situations.

If you are assessing in the workplace you should involve your learners by discussing what will be assessed, how and when. This would enable a two-way conversation leading to an appropriate plan of action for further training and/or formal assessments to take place. You could also ask your learners to complete a SWOT (strengths, weaknesses, opportunities and threats) analysis. This would give them the opportunity to consider their current skills, knowledge and understanding and how it relates to their progress and development.

Depending upon the topic you are assessing, there are different ways of involving your learner by the use of questions. If you are assessing informally, for example, asking questions during a session, you could start with an open question and then move on to a hypothetical question if you are not getting the response you expected. If you are formally assessing a learner for a practical skill, you could ask them some open questions to check their knowledge and understanding. If you are asking questions to a group, make sure you give everyone the chance to answer, not just those who are keen to answer first. If possible, ask a question to everyone in the group, this enables all individuals to be included and involved.

You could regularly ask your learners how they feel they are progressing: hopefully they will identify any issues before you need to tell them. Sometimes, learners are unsure of what they have achieved and what they need to do to progress further. Asking them to reflect upon their progress can be a useful way of linking it towards the programme or qualification they are aiming to achieve.

Q44 Explain why it is important to involve others in the assessment process.

Your response could explain that it's important to involve and communicate with others not only to make sure learners are fully supported, but to ensure the assessment process is effective and that learning has taken place. It will also ensure that everyone who has an interest in the learner knows how they are progressing and what they have achieved. For example, you may need to liaise with administrators who will register learners for a qualification, and with internal quality assurers who will be monitoring your assessment activities.

At some point, you might need to liaise with others regarding any particular learner requirements to ensure consistency of support. For example, you might have a learner who would benefit from a different assessment method, i.e. oral questions instead of written questions. You might therefore need to liaise with the awarding organisation to ensure this is acceptable. You could have a learner who would prefer to be assessed bilingually, and you would therefore need to contact another member of staff who could help. Internal contacts can include: administrators, colleagues and support staff.

If you are liaising with external contacts, you should remain professional at all times as you are representing your organisation. People might not always remember your name; however, you will be known as *that person from XYZ organisation*. You therefore need to create a good and lasting impression of yourself and your organisation. You should also remember aspects of confidentiality and data protection, and keep notes of all activities in case you need to refer to them again. External contacts can include careers advisers, external quality assurers and workplace supervisors.

If you are currently teaching, you could produce a case study of how you have involved learners and others in the assessment process.

> 2.2 Explain the role and use of peer and self assessment in the assessment process

Q45 What is the role of peer and self assessment?

Your response could state that peer assessment involves a learner assessing another learner's progress. Self assessment involves a learner assessing their own progress. Both methods encourage learners to make decisions about what has been learnt so far, take responsibility for their learning, get involved with the assessment process and give feedback.

Q46 Explain how peer and self assessment can be used with learners in the assessment process.

Your response could explain that peer and self assessment actively involves learners; however, you would need to ensure everyone was aware of the criteria to be assessed, how to reach a decision and give feedback.

Peer assessment can be useful to develop and motivate learners. However, this should be managed carefully, as you may have some learners who do not get along and might use the opportunity to demoralise one another. You would need to give advice to your learners as to how to give feedback effectively. If learner feedback is given skilfully, other learners may think more about what their peers have said than about what you have said. If you consider peer assessment has a valuable contribution to make to the assessment process, ensure you plan for it to enable your learners to become accustomed and more proficient at giving it. However, the final decision as to learner achievement will lie with you.

Ways of using peer assessment include:

- assessing each other's work anonymously and giving written or verbal feedback
- giving grades and/or written or verbal feedback regarding individual presentations
- holding group discussions before collectively agreeing a grade and giving feedback, perhaps for a group presentation
- suggesting improvements to their peers' work
- writing a written statement of how their peers could improve

You could then explain that self assessment involves a learner assessing their own progress, which can lead to them setting their own goals. It can give responsibility and ownership of their progress and achievements. However, learners might feel they have achieved more than they actually have: therefore, you will still need to confirm their achievements, or otherwise.

Ways of using self assessment include:

- awarding a grade for a presentation they have delivered
- suggesting improvements regarding their skills and knowledge
- compiling a written statement of how they could improve their work

---

2.3 Identify sources of information that should be made available to learners and others involved in the assessment process

---

Q47 List at least four sources of information which will prove beneficial to learners and others who are involved in the assessment process.

Your list could include some of the following:

- the standards or units to be assessed
- achievement records
- assessment documentation such as plans and feedback records
- internet websites and journals
- progress records
- resources such as text books
- tutorial reviews

Your learners will need information such as copies of assessment documents to enable them to know what will be assessed, and feedback records to enable them to know how they are progressing and what they have achieved.

If you need to liaise with others who have an involvement with your learners, they will need certain information to help them support the learner and the assessment process. Communicating regularly will ensure everyone who is involved with your learner is familiar with any support requirements, and knows of their progress and achievement.

When communicating any personal information to others, you will need to follow your organisation's confidentiality procedures and any requirements regarding data protection.

Q48 Identify where the sources of information can be located.

You could identify where you would locate the information. For example:

- the standards or units to be assessed: the awarding organisation website

- achievement records: filing cabinet in the staff office, or electronic files

- assessment documentation: filing cabinet in the staff office, or electronic files

- internet websites and journals: notice board in the class room or workshop, and in the learner handbook

- progress records: filing cabinet in the staff office, or electronic files

- resources such as text books: library, class room, workshop or learning resources centre

- tutorial reviews: filing cabinet in the staff office, or electronic files

Theory focus

References and further information

Gravells, A (2013) *The Award in Education and Training.* London: Learning Matters SAGE.

Murphy, P (2005) *Learners, Learning and Assessment.* London: SAGE Publications Ltd.

Read, H (2011) *The Best Assessor's Guide. Bideford:* Read On Publications.

Read, H (2013) *The Best Initial Assessment Guide. Bideford:* Read On Publications.

Tummons, J (2011) *Assessing Learning in the Lifelong Learning Sector* (3rd Edn). Exeter: Learning Matters.

Websites

Data Protection Act – www.legislation.gov.uk/ukpga/1998/29/contents

Initial assessment – http://archive.excellencegateway.org.uk/page.aspx?o=108146

Assessment methods – www.brookes.ac.uk/services/ocsld/resources/methods.html

UNIT TITLE: Understanding assessment in education and training
Assessment Grid

Learning outcomes The learner will:	Assessment criteria The learner can:	Example evidence
2. Understand how to involve learners and others in the assessment process	2.1 Explain why it is important to involve learners and others in the assessment process	An explanation of why it is important to involve your learners in the assessment process. For example, to give learners the opportunity to inform you of anything which might affect their progress and/or achievement. An explanation of why it is important to involve others in the assessment process. For example, administrators who will register learners for a qualification. A case study of how you have involved learners and others in the assessment process (anonymised).
	2.2 Explain the role and use of peer and self assessment in the assessment process	An explanation of the role of peer and self assessment in the assessment process such as peer assessment involves a learner assessing another learner's progress. Self assessment involves a learner assessing their own progress. An explanation of how peer assessment can be used with learners. For example, learners assessing each other's work anonymously and giving written or verbal feedback. An explanation of how self assessment can be used with learners. For example, a learner awarding a grade for a presentation they have delivered.
	2.3 Identify sources of information that should be made available to learners and others involved in the assessment process	A list of sources of information which will prove beneficial to learners and others who are involved in the assessment process. For example, the standards to be assessed, assessment plans and feedback records, progress and achievement records. An identification of where the information can be located such as: the standards to be assessed would be accessible on the awarding organisation's website, achievement records will be in a filing cabinet in the staff office, or as electronic files.

This chapter is in two parts. The first part, **Self assessment activities**, contains questions and activities which relate to the third learning outcome of the Award in Education and Training unit **Understanding assessment in education and training.**

The assessment criteria are shown in boxes and are followed by questions and activities for you to carry out. Ensure your responses are *specific to you*, the *subject* you will teach and the *context* and *environment* in which you will teach.

After completing the activities, check your responses with the second part: **Guidance for evidencing achievement**. This guidance is not intended to give you the answers to questions you may be asked in any formal assessments; however, it will help you focus your responses towards meeting the assessment criteria.

At the end of the chapter is an example of a completed **Assessment Grid**, which gives ideas for evidence you could provide towards meeting the assessment criteria. Evidence can be cross-referenced between units and assessment criteria if it meets the requirements.

Self assessment activities

> 3.1 Describe key features of constructive feedback

Q49 What does the term constructive feedback mean?

Q50 Describe the key features of giving constructive feedback.

> 3.2 Explain how constructive feedback contributes to the assessment process

Q51 Explain how constructive feedback can contribute to the assessment process.

> 3.3 Explain ways to give constructive feedback to learners

Q52 Explain ways of giving constructive feedback to your learners.

Guidance for evidencing achievement

3.1 Describe key features of constructive feedback

Q49 What does the term constructive feedback mean?

Your response could explain that constructive feedback is about conveying your assessment decision to your learner in a way that helps reassure, boost confidence, encourage and motivate them. All learners need to know how they are progressing, and what they have achieved, therefore giving feedback in a constructive way will help them realise this.

The decisions you make regarding your learners' progress can affect them both personally and professionally. It's therefore important to remain factual about what you have assessed and to be objective with your judgements. You should not be subjective and let other aspects influence or compromise your decision. For example, passing a learner just because you like them, feel they have worked hard or are under pressure to meet certain targets.

Q50 Describe the key features of giving constructive feedback.

Your response could describe key features such as:

- Using your learner's name as this makes the feedback more personal.

- Asking your learner how they feel they have done, before telling them. For example, if you have just observed them perform a task and they made a mistake, it gives them the opportunity to say so before you need to, providing they have realised it.

- Giving specific feedback regarding what was and what wasn't achieved to enable your learner to know what they have done, and what they might need to do to improve.

- Making feedback a two-way process. This allows a discussion to take place to clarify any points, and enables you both to ask questions and clarify points.

- Watching your own and your learner's body language. If you are giving verbal feedback, be aware of aspects such as movement, facial expressions and the tone of your voice. Watch your learner too and follow signals such as a furrowed brow which might indicate they haven't understood something.

- Setting new targets or action points, with clear dates for achievement. If you need to do this, make sure your learner fully understands what needs to be done and by when. Check how they are progressing nearer to the agreed date and give support and guidance as necessary.

3.2 Explain how constructive feedback contributes to the assessment process

Q51 Explain how constructive feedback can contribute to the assessment process.

Your response could explain that giving feedback in a constructive way enables your learners to know what progress they have made, which requirements they have achieved, and any action that may be required. This contributes to the assessment process by ensuring everyone is aware of what has been achieved, and what might still need to be done.

Asking your learner how they feel they have done, before telling them, enables them to contribute towards their own self assessment of progress and achievement.

Constructive feedback creates opportunities for clarification and discussion, and emphasises progress rather than failure. It helps improve confidence and motivation, and identifies further learning opportunities. Always check that any action points which have been agreed with your learner have been met by the target date. This shows that you have not forgotten what your learner is working towards.

3.3 Explain ways to give constructive feedback to learners

Q52 Explain ways of giving constructive feedback to your learners.

Your response could explain that you could give constructive feedback in the following ways:

- Formally, i.e. in writing, or informally, i.e. verbally. This should always be given at a level which is appropriate for each learner. Feedback should be more thorough than just a quick comment such as *well done*. It should be given in a constructive way and include specific facts which relate to progress, achievement or otherwise, in order to help your learners develop. If you are giving written or electronic feedback consider that how your learner reads it may not be how you intended it.

- Directly, i.e. to an individual, or indirectly, i.e. to a group. When giving feedback to an individual, make sure you are specific about what has and what has not been achieved. If you are giving feedback to a group, make sure you identify what each individual has achieved.

- Being descriptive rather than evaluative. This way lets you describe what your learner has done, how they have met the requirements and what they can do to progress further. It enables you to provide opportunities for your learner to make any adjustments or improvements to reach a particular standard. Feedback should never just be an evaluative statement like *Well done*, or *That's great, you've passed*. This doesn't tell your learner what was done well, or was great about it. Your learner will be pleased to know they have passed; however, they won't have anything to build upon for the future.

- Using the *praise sandwich*. When giving feedback it can really help your learner to hear first what they have done well, followed by what they need to improve, and then end on a positive note to keep them motivated. Often, the word *but* is used to link these points; replacing this with the word *however* can make it much easier for your learner to accept.

Theory focus

References and further information

Gravells, A (2013) *The Award in Education and Training*. London: Learning Matters SAGE.

Murphy, P (2005) *Learners, Learning and Assessment*. London: SAGE Publications Ltd.

Read, H (2011) *The Best Assessor's Guide*. Bideford: Read On Publications.

Tummons, J (2011) *Assessing Learning in the Lifelong Learning Sector* (3rd Edn). Exeter: Learning Matters.

Websites

Developing Assessment Feedback – http://escalate.ac.uk/4147

Giving feedback – www.ehow.com/how_2173337_give-feedback.html

UNIT TITLE: Understanding assessment in education and training
Assessment Grid

Learning outcomes The learner will:	Assessment criteria The learner can:	Example evidence
3. Understand the role and use of constructive feedback in the assessment process	3.1 Describe key features of constructive feedback	An explanation of what constructive feedback means. For example, conveying your decision to your learner in a way that helps reassure, boost confidence, encourage and motivate them. A description of the key features of constructive feedback. For example, using your learner's name; asking your learner how they feel they have done, before telling them; making the feedback a two-way process; watching your own and your learner's body language; setting new targets or action points, with clear dates for achievement.
	3.2 Explain how constructive feedback contributes to the assessment process	An explanation of how constructive feedback contributes to the assessment process. For example, enabling learners to know what progress they have made, which requirements they have achieved, and any action that may be required; creating opportunities for clarification and discussion, emphasising progress rather than failure, helping improve confidence and motivation, identifying further learning opportunities.
	3.3 Explain ways to give constructive feedback to learners	An explanation of ways of giving constructive feedback. For example, formally, i.e. in writing, or informally, i.e. verbally; directly, i.e. to an individual, or indirectly, i.e. to a group; being descriptive rather than evaluative; using the praise sandwich.

12 UNDERSTAND REQUIREMENTS FOR KEEPING RECORDS OF ASSESSMENT IN EDUCATION AND TRAINING

This chapter is in two parts. The first part, *Self assessment activities*, contains questions and activities which relate to the fourth learning outcome of the Award in Education and Training unit *Understanding assessment in education and training*.

The assessment criteria are shown in boxes and are followed by questions and activities for you to carry out. Ensure your responses are *specific to you*, the *subject* you will teach and the *context* and *environment* in which you will teach.

After completing the activities, check your responses with the second part: *Guidance for evidencing achievement*. This guidance is not intended to give you the answers to questions you may be asked in any formal assessments; however, it will help you focus your responses towards meeting the assessment criteria.

At the end of the chapter is an example of a completed *Assessment Grid,* which gives ideas for evidence you could provide towards meeting the assessment criteria. Evidence can be cross-referenced between units and assessment criteria if it meets the requirements.

Self assessment activities

> 4.1 Explain the need to keep records of assessment of learning

Q53 List at least four assessment records that a teacher could keep.

Q54 Explain why there is a need to use and keep records of assessment.

> 4.2 Summarise the requirements for keeping records of assessment in an organisation

Q55 Summarise the requirements for keeping records of assessment in an organisation.

Guidance for evidencing achievement

4.1 Explain the need to keep records of assessment of learning

Q53 List at least four assessment records that a teacher could keep.

Your list could include some of the following:

- achievement dates and grades
- action plans
- appeals records
- application forms
- assessment plan and review records
- assessment tracking sheet showing progression through a qualification for all learners
- authentication declarations/statements
- checklists
- copies of certificates
- diagnostic test results
- enrolment forms
- formative and summative records
- feedback records
- initial assessment records
- learning preference results
- observation checklists
- observation reports
- performance and knowledge records
- professional discussion records
- progress reports
- receipts for assignments handed in
- records of achievement
- records of oral questions and responses
- retention and achievement records
- standardisation records
- tutorial reviews
- witness testimonies

Q54 Explain why there is a need to use and keep records of assessment.

Your response could explain that records of assessment must be used and kept to show an audit trail of your learners' progress from commencement to completion. If a learner loses their work, without any assessment records you have nothing to show what was assessed and what was achieved. Records are usually kept at an organisation for three years in case they are needed at any point after a learner has left.

Records must be up to date, accurate, factual and legible whether they are stored manually or electronically. If you are saving to a computer, always ensure you have a backup copy in case any data is lost. You must always maintain confidentiality and follow relevant legislation such as the Data Protection Act (1998), which is mandatory for all organisations that hold or process personal data. Confidentially of certain information should also be followed. Keeping full and accurate factual records is also necessary in case a learner appeals against an assessment decision or a dispute occurs, for example regarding plagiarism.

If you are currently teaching, you could include examples of assessment records you have used with your learners (anonymised).

4.2 Summarise the requirements for keeping records of assessment in an organisation

Q55 Summarise the requirements for keeping records of assessment in an organisation.

Your response could summarise an organisation's own requirements, as well as those of external bodies, and those required by legislation.

Organisational requirements might include keeping records such as: appeals; assessment policies; achievement statistics, progression data and quality assurance information. These are all needed to prove what assessment activities have taken place and what has been achieved by individual learners. Records of quality assurance help ensure the assessment process is accurate, fair, consistent and reliable.

External body requirements might include keeping records required by regulators such as Ofsted, who will need to see learners' progress and achievements. If you are assessing a qualification which is accredited by an awarding organisation, they will have requirements which must be met to ensure you are planning and carrying out assessments correctly. External quality assurers will visit organisations and will need to see records of assessment and internal quality assurance activities. This is to ensure decisions have been made accurately and fairly, and that their requirements have been met.

Legislative requirements could include the Data Protection Act (1998), the Equality Act (2010), the Freedom of Information Act (2000) and the Health and Safety at Work etc Act (1974).

The Data Protection Act (1998) made provision for the regulation of the processing of information relating to individuals, including the obtaining, holding, use or disclosure of such information. It was amended in 2003 to include electronic data.

The Equality Act (2010) replaced all previous anti-discrimination legislation and consolidated it into one act (England, Scotland and Wales). It provides rights for people not to be directly discriminated against or harassed because they have an association with a disabled person or because they are wrongly perceived as disabled.

The Freedom of Information Act (2000) gives learners the opportunity to request to see the information public bodies hold about them.

The Health and Safety at Work etc Act (1974) imposes obligations on all staff within an organisation commensurate with their role and responsibility. Risk assessments should be carried out where necessary. In the event of an accident, particularly one resulting in death or serious injury, an investigation by the Health and Safety Executive may result in the prosecution of individuals found to be negligent as well as the organisation.

Theory focus

References and further information

Gravells, A (2013) *The Award in Education and Training.* London: Learning Matters SAGE.

Read, H (2011) *The Best Assessor's Guide.* Bideford: Read On Publications.

Tummons, J (2011) *Assessing Learning in the Lifelong Learning Sector* (3rd Edn). Exeter: Learning Matters.

Websites

Government legislation – www.legislation.gov.uk

Ofsted – www.ofsted.gov.uk

Plagiarism – www.plagiarism.org and www.plagiarismadvice.org

Regulatory requirements – http://standards.gov/regulations.cfm

UNIT TITLE: Understanding assessment in education and training
Assessment Grid

Learning outcomes The learner will:	Assessment criteria The learner can:	Example evidence
4. Understand requirements for keeping records of assessment in education and training	4.1 Explain the need to keep records of assessment of learning	A list of assessment records, such as: action plans; achievement dates and grades; feedback records; tracking sheets. An explanation of the need to keep records of assessment. For example, to provide an audit trail; to know what has been achieved by whom; in case of an appeal or dispute. Examples of actual assessment records used with learners (anonymised).
	4.2 Summarise the requirements for keeping records of assessment in an organisation	A summary of the requirements for keeping records in an organisation. For example, the organisation's own requirements, those of external bodies, and those required by legislation.

In this chapter you will learn about:

- the micro-teach session
- planning to deliver your session
- facilitating your session
- assessing learning
- giving and receiving feedback
- evaluating your session
- micro-teach checklist

This chapter will assist you in preparation for your micro-teach session whether pre-service or in-service. A shortened version of this chapter appears in Gravells (2013) *The Award in Education and Training*.

A micro-teach checklist, and a list of useful references, further information and website links can be found at the end of the chapter.

The micro-teach session

To achieve the Award in Education and Training you need to demonstrate your skills, knowledge and understanding as a teacher or trainer. You are therefore required to facilitate a short session with learners, known as a micro-teach session, and then evaluate your practice. This might be to your peers if you are pre-service (not currently teaching) or to your current learners if you are in-service (currently teaching). This gives you the opportunity to put theory into practice, and will usually be for a minimum of 15 or 30 minutes. You might also need to partake in your peers' micro-teach sessions by being one of their learners and/or observing how they facilitate their session. The date, time and place will be agreed in advance and you will be assessed by an observer who will make notes and/or use an observation checklist to ensure you meet all the criteria. You may find it useful to see the checklist in advance as it will help you know what they are looking for. Your observer might make a visual recording of your session which you can view afterwards to help you evaluate how you performed. This will enable you to see things you were not aware of: for example, saying *erm,* using a lot of hand gestures, or not using enough eye contact with your learners. You should be told in advance if you are going to be visually recorded; try not to be put off by it, but embrace it as a way of developing yourself further.

The micro-teach session is a learning experience for you and a chance to put all your new-found knowledge into practice. You may feel nervous, which is quite normal. However, try to imagine you are acting a role and this should help boost your confidence and calm your nerves. You are the teacher in this situation; you need to be in control and not let any personal issues affect you. If you are organised with a detailed session plan, and you have checked the room and equipment in advance, hopefully you won't encounter any problems. Try to relax, but stay focused and above all enjoy yourself. As you will have prepared your session carefully, your delivery should follow logically through the introduction, development and summary stages.

Deciding what to deliver

You might be required to deliver the subject you wish to teach, or you might be able to deliver anything you wish such as a hobby or something that interests you. It might be an academic topic such as identifying key dates in history, a vocational topic such as creating a hairstyle, or something else such as folding napkins, icing cup cakes, or creating a hanging basket. Whatever subject you choose to deliver, you will need to carefully plan what you will be doing, what your learners will be doing and how long the activities will take. You must also assess that learning has taken place.

If you are unsure about what to deliver, have a chat in advance with your observer. They might be able to help you with some ideas to get you thinking about a suitable subject. Table 13.1 lists some topics that people have used for their micro-teach session in the past. Looking at the list might give you some ideas.

**Table 13.1 Some topics used by people in the past
for their micro-teach sessions**

Aromatherapy	Creating a hanging basket	Interpreting road signs
Astrology	Creative writing	Kite making
Astronomy	Dog grooming	Manual handling
Backgammon	Drawing a portrait	Map reading
Ballroom dancing	Fire prevention	Origami
Bandaging	First aid	Poetry
Basic dance moves	Folding napkins	Reflexology
Basket weaving	Food hygiene	Salsa dancing
Bird watching	Hand massage	Using a digital camera
Calligraphy	Historical key dates	Using search engines
Control and restraint	How to eat healthily	Wine tasting
Creating a hair style	Icing cup cakes	Zumba dancing

To help you prepare for your session, you might find it useful to ask your observer the following questions:

- How long will my session be?

- When and where will it take place?

- Who will observe me and will they make a visual recording?

- Will you need to see my session plan in advance?

- What if I change my mind about what I'm going to deliver?

- Is my topic appropriate for my learners?

- How should I dress?

- What equipment, resources and computer programs are available for me to use?

- How many people will I be delivering to?

- How can I find out their learning preferences, any individual needs, and prior knowledge and/or experience of the subject?

- Can I show a video clip? If so, how long can it be?

- Will I have internet access?

- What will I need to bring with me, e.g. board markers, a clock, spare pens?

- Can I arrive early to set up the area, e.g. move anything, check resources and equipment?

- If I use a presentation, should I e-mail it to you or bring it on a memory stick?

- Is there somewhere I can get handouts photocopied in advance?

- Should I start with an icebreaker and ground rules?

- What kind of assessment activity should I use?

- How will I receive feedback afterwards?

- Is there a form I need to complete to evaluate my session?

Pre-service micro-teach session
As a pre-service teacher or trainer without learners of your own, you will usually be delivering to a group of your peers who will become your learners for the micro-teach session. This might be the first time you have taught a group of people and your peers will probably be very encouraging and supportive. If you have chosen to deliver a subject you know well, your knowledge should help your confidence.

You will probably be in the same environment you have been learning in, or a central meeting point if you have been studying through a distance learning programme. Hopefully you will have met your peers previously and feel comfortable with them; if not, it would be useful to talk to them beforehand to help everyone relax. If you are due to deliver your session after someone else, you will probably be thinking about your own delivery rather than focusing upon theirs. Try not to do this: as well as making yourself feel more nervous, you might not participate in your peer's session effectively, making it harder for them to deliver. You might also miss some good approaches and ideas.

Alternatively, depending upon how many are in your peer group, you might be able to miss the session before yours to carry out final preparations for your own session. Being well prepared and having self-confidence and knowledge of your subject should help alleviate any worries. It's likely your learners will have less knowledge of your topic and therefore be keen to learn and get involved.

In-service teaching session
If you are currently teaching or training, you will be classed as in-service, and might be able to deliver a session to your own learners in your usual environment.

As you already have some experience of teaching or training, delivering a session to your own learners should be fairly straightforward. Your session might last longer than the time your observer will be present; they might therefore miss the beginning or ending and arrive part way through. You should try to plan the session to allow time to talk to your observer either before or after. This will enable you to discuss your delivery, justify any aspects they have missed and to receive feedback.

You may want to introduce the observer to your learners and state they are observing you, not them. Depending upon the age of your learners, having a stranger in the room might lead to some behaviour issues. If so, you must deal with these as soon as they arise and act professionally at all times.

If you are in-service, it is possible to take one of the units from the Learning and Development qualification:

* Facilitate learning and development for individuals OR

* Facilitate learning and development in groups

instead of the Award in Education and Training unit which relates to micro-teaching called *Understanding and using inclusive approaches in education and training*. If you are taking either of the Learning and Development units, you must be observed with your own learners and meet all the assessment criteria of the unit.

Planning to deliver your session

Once you know which subject you will deliver, you will need to create a plan, often known as a *teaching and learning plan* or *session plan*. This should have a clear *aim* (what you want your learners to achieve), which is then broken down into *objectives* (how your learners will achieve your aim). Your plan should show what you expect your learners to achieve expressed in a way that will enable you to determine that learning has taken place. For example, your learners might *explain*, and/or *demonstrate* something. Your observer will probably want to see your plan well in advance to give you advice and support. Knowing whether you are delivering a practical session, i.e. skills, or a theory session, i.e. knowledge and understanding, will help you choose appropriate objectives at the right level for your learners. See Table 13.2 for some examples of objectives at different levels.

Objectives should always be SMART to enable you to deliver and assess learning effectively. This is an acronym for:

- **S**pecific – are the objectives clearly defined and stated to meet the required outcomes?

- **M**easurable – can they be achieved at the right level?

- **A**chievable – can they be met by all learners?

- **R**elevant – do they relate to the aim, the subject, and the learners?

- **T**ime bound – can agreed targets and timings be met?

Your session should have a beginning (the introduction), a middle section (the development) and an ending (the summary/conclusion) which should show a logical progression of learning and assessment. Timings should be allocated to each of the activities you plan to use and you should not be speaking for the majority of the session. Remember that it's more important what your learners are doing than what you are doing. Try and use a mixture of teaching, learning and assessment activities to ensure your learners are active, not passive. See Table 13.3 for an example session plan for a 30-minute micro-teach session.

Once you have your plan, you will need to prepare all the activities, handouts, resources, presentations and assessment activities you intend to use. You may need to learn how to use something in advance: for example, if you wish to use a computerised presentation during your session or link to the internet via an interactive whiteboard. You should check all presentations and handouts for spelling, grammar, punctuation and sentence construction errors and ensure text and pictures positively represent all aspects of equality and diversity. If you are delivering a 30-minute session and you plan to show a video for ten minutes, this will not demonstrate how teaching and learning is taking place. Videos are good for visual learners, but if used, keep them short or you may lose the attention of other learners.

Carry out a trial run with friends or family to check your timings. You might find that what you planned to cover in 30 minutes takes only 20. Time will go quickly during your micro-teach session, particularly if you are asked lots of questions. Make sure you have all the necessary equipment, resources and stationery you may need. A clock or a watch in a visible place will help you keep track of time. Try to have a contingency plan in case anything goes wrong: for example, a hard copy of an electronic presentation.

If possible check in advance and/or arrive early to see that everything is available and working in the room you will be in. You may want to rearrange the area beforehand to suit your subject and to enable everyone to see and hear you. You might find your peers are willing to help with this. You may need to bring two copies of your plan, one for yourself and one for your observer. Time for setting up and clearing away afterwards should be outside of your observed time, although you should prepare so that this can be done as quickly and efficiently as possible.

Table 13.2 Objectives at different levels

Level	Skills		Knowledge and understanding	
Foundation	Attempt	Listen	Answer	Repeat
	Carry out	Read	Match	Show
	Learn		Recall	
1	Arrange	Switch	Access	Name
	Help	Use	Know	Recap
	Imitate	View	List	Recognise
	Obtain	Watch	Locate	State
2	Assist	Perform	Compare	Reorder
	Change	Practise	Describe	Select
	Choose	Prepare	Identify	Write
	Connect	Present		
	Demonstrate	Rearrange		
	Draw			
3	Apply	Devise	Compose	Paraphrase
	Assemble	Estimate	Explain	Test
	Assess	Facilitate		
	Build	Illustrate		
	Create	Make		
	Construct	Measure		
	Design	Produce		
4	Calculate	Modify	Analyse	Revise
	Complete	Plan	Invent	Summarise
	Convert	Quality assure	Contextualise	Verify
	Diagnose	Research	Outline	
	Explore	Search		
	Generate	Solve		
	Maintain			
5	Accept responsibility	Interview	Categorise	Evaluate
	Encapsulate	Manage	Classify	Interpret
	Establish	Organise	Contrast	
		Teach		
6	Operate	Utilise	Extrapolate	Translate
			Synthesise	
7	Modify		Strategise	
8	Lead		Redefine	

Table 13.3 Example teaching and learning plan (session plan) for a 30-minute micro-teach session

Teacher/trainer	A N Other	Date	09 October	Venue	Room 5
Subject/level Qualification reference	Communication Skills Level 3 Unit 010	Time Duration	6 p.m. 30 minutes	Number of learners	9
Aim of session	To introduce learners to non-verbal communication skills				
Group composition	6 male and 3 female aged 24–64 A mixture of learning preferences therefore a variety of approaches and activities will be used Jenny has dyslexia therefore the handout will be printed on pastel paper for all learners, and also available electronically Magda is diabetic and may need to leave the room to take insulin				

Timing	Objectives/Learning outcomes: Learners will:	Teacher activities	Learner activities	Resources	Assessment activities
5 mins	Listen to the introduction, aim and objectives	Introduce self, explain aim and objectives Ask if anyone has any prior knowledge or experience of non-verbal communication skills	Listen, respond and ask questions	Flipchart	Oral questions
8 mins	State methods of non-verbal communication	Explain different methods of non-verbal communication and facilitate group activity	Listen and make notes, then take part in an activity in groups of three (mixed learning preferences) to demonstrate body language and state methods used	Paper and pens PowerPoint slides 1 and 2	Oral questions Observation Discussion
5 mins	Identify aspects of good and bad body language	Explain and demonstrate appropriate (good) and inappropriate (bad) body language signals Ask individual questions using the pose, pause, pick (PPP) method (remove if short of time)	Discuss, listen, offer opinions and identify aspects of body language (reduce discussion time if overrunning) Answer oral questions (if time)	PowerPoint slide 3	Oral questions Observation Discussion
8 mins	Discuss experiences regarding assumptions made from body language	Discuss assumptions and give handout Issue written questions Give answers to questions	Look at handout (pictures of body language) and discuss with group Individually answer written questions and mark responses	PowerPoint slide 4 Handout 1	Discussion Written questions and answers
4 mins	Listen to the recap Ask questions State what they have learnt from the session (if time)	Summarise the session, relate to the aim and objectives on the flipchart If time, ask if anyone has any further questions Thank the learners for their contributions	Listen to the summary, ask questions (If spare time – each learner to state one significant point they have learnt from the session)	PowerPoint slide 5 Handout 2 Flipchart	Oral questions

Facilitating your session

You should be able to facilitate your session logically through the introduction, development and summary/conclusion stages.

Introduction

Before you speak, take a few deep breaths, smile at your learners and use eye contact with everyone; this should help you to relax. You can then introduce yourself by saying *Hello, my name is ...,* followed by your topic aim and objectives. You might like to keep these on display throughout your session, perhaps on a piece of flipchart paper on the wall or as a handout. Don't tell your learners if you are nervous as it probably won't show. Be aware of your posture, speak a little more loudly and slowly than normal as being anxious or nervous may make you speak softly or quickly. Even if you feel you are shaking, it is highly likely no one will notice. If your mind suddenly goes blank, take a couple of deep breaths for a few seconds and look at your plan to help you refocus; it might seem a long time to you but it won't to your learners. You will need to establish a rapport with your learners and engage and interact with them from the start. Asking the question *What experience, if any, do you have of ...?* is a good way of involving your learners in your subject from the start and helps you check any prior learning. Make sure you communicate effectively with everyone and ensure you can meet any individual needs.

Keep your plan handy as a prompt. If you feel you might forget something, use a highlight pen beforehand to mark key words which you can quickly look at. Standing rather than sitting might help your confidence and voice projection. Keep things simple, don't complicate things or try to deliver too much too quickly. Conversely, don't expect too much from your learners, as your subject may be very new to them. If this is the first time you have met your learners, you might want to carry out a short icebreaker with them or ask them to introduce themselves to you if you have time. If your peer group know each other, they will be familiar with the ground rules and other requirements such as the fire procedure. You might like to encourage your learners to ask questions if they need to clarify any points at any time.

Development

You should develop your session by using a variety of teaching and learning approaches to reach all learning preferences and to keep your learners motivated. Summarise and recap regularly to reinforce your points. Assessment should take place at key points, for example, by asking open questions to check knowledge (ones that begin with *who, what, when, where, why* and *how*). Try to use names when talking to your learners and if possible address everyone in the group; don't just focus on a particular learner who you know can give you the correct answers. Having your learners' names written down in advance will help. Try to use the PPP (Pose, Pause, Pick) method when asking questions. If you have a small group, you could plan to ask one open question of each learner.

The timing of activities needs to be followed carefully; if you are only delivering a 15-minute session you may not have time for group activities. If you do set activities, think what you will be doing while your learners are working: i.e. moving around them and observing or asking questions shows you are in control. Longer sessions benefit from a mixture of teaching and learning approaches and different assessment activities. Don't forget to keep assessing that learning is taking place. If you have delivered a practical task, you will need to observe that your learners can demonstrate what you have taught, and have the required knowledge to carry it out.

Summary/conclusion

You need to summarise or conclude your session in a succinct way and relate it back to your topic aim and objectives. If you have time, you can summarise learning with a short quiz or multiple-choice test which is a good way to check knowledge and understanding. You might like to ask your learners if they have any questions. However, you may be met with silence, or they might have lots of questions which will then impact upon your time. If you find you have covered everything and have spare time, you could ask each member of the group to state *one significant thing* they feel they have learnt from the session. This is a good way of filling in spare time if necessary, and shows you what each individual learner has learnt. You could issue a handout at the end which summarises your session and gives further information such as relevant text books and websites. Don't forget to explain why you are issuing it, otherwise learners might get confused. If you issue a handout during the session which is not relevant at the time, your learners will look at it and might not focus on you or the topic.

If you are unsure of how to end your session, simply say *Thank you, I've enjoyed my session with you today,* this will indicate to your group you have finished. Make sure you tidy the area afterwards. Don't say something like *That's it, I've finished now* as it's not very professional.

Assessing learning

At some point during your micro-teach session, you will need to assess that learning has taken place by each individual. You will probably not be using formal assessment activities, as your learners might not be taking a qualification (unless you are an in-service teacher with your own learners). You therefore need to use informal assessment activities to ensure learning has been successful. The following are some assessment activities you could use with your learners depending upon the level of learning:

- completing gapped handouts or word searches
- discussions in pairs or groups
- group tasks
- questions – written or oral
- multiple-choice questions

- observation of a practical task
- puzzles
- quizzes
- role plays

You might assess as you progress through your session by asking questions, for example using the PPP technique. If you are using this technique, make sure you have a different question for everyone in the group. If you have demonstrated a practical topic, make sure everyone has the opportunity to have a go and that you can observe them doing it. Depending upon the level of learning, you could use a gapped handout and issue this at an appropriate time. A gapped handout is a page of text with missing words which the learners have to complete. Quizzes, puzzles and word searches can be fun and be completed individually, in pairs or groups. However, any assessment activities which are carried out in pairs or groups must enable you to make a decision as to each individual's achievement.

Once you have assessed that learning has taken place, you need to give feedback to your learners in a constructive way. If you don't, they won't know if they have been successful or not. Don't forget that assessment should not be in isolation from the teaching and learning process.

Giving and receiving feedback

Throughout your time attending the Award programme you may have been carrying out various activities with your peers, delivering short presentations and giving each other feedback. You might have delivered some mini sessions and received feedback from your teacher as well as your peers. Sometimes, your peers may be more negative when giving you feedback as they are not yet skilled at being constructive. Try not to take any negative comments personally, your peers are just saying what they see; and hopefully their feedback skills will improve over time. Alternatively, you might feel the feedback from your peers is quite helpful.

Feedback should always include something positive or constructive, as well as stating any areas for development. Feedback which is negative can be unhelpful and hurtful if not given skilfully.

Different feedback methods include:

- descriptive – giving examples of what could be improved and why, this can be written or verbal, and is usually formal

- evaluative – statements such as *well done* or *good*. This method does not offer helpful or constructive advice; it can be written or verbal, and is usually informal

Descriptive feedback lets you describe *what* has been done, *how* it has been achieved and *what* needs to be done to progress further. It enables you to provide opportunities for learners to make any adjustments or improvements to reach a particular standard.

Evaluative feedback might be good to hear, for example, *well done Pete*; however, it does not give the learner any opportunity to know *what* was done well or *how* they could improve.

Giving feedback

Giving feedback is a part of achieving the Award and you may find it hard to do at first. You should give feedback during your micro-teach session to your learners when you have assessed an activity or asked a question.

When giving feedback to others you need to be aware it could affect their self-esteem. The quality of feedback received can be a key factor in their progress and the ability to learn new skills. Ongoing constructive feedback, which has been carefully thought through, is an indication of your interest in the person and of your intention to help them develop and do well in the future.

You might be required to give feedback to your peers after they have delivered their micro-teach sessions. If so, try and follow this example:

- Own your statements by using the word 'I' rather than 'you'

- Begin with something positive, for example, '*I really liked the confident manner in which you delivered your session*'

- You could then ask the person how they felt their session went, for example, '*what do you think your strengths and areas for development are?*' They may have noticed some aspects which need improvement, if so, this saves you having to be too critical

- Be specific about what you have seen, for example, '*I felt the way you explained your topic was really interesting due to your knowledge and humour*' or '*I found the way you explained your topic was rather confusing to me*'

- Offer constructive, specific or developmental follow-on points, for example, '*I feel I would have understood it better if you had broken the topic down into smaller stages*'

- End with something positive, for example, '*I enjoyed your session, you had prepared well and you came across as very organised and professional*'

Being constructive, specific and developmental with what you say, and owning your statements should help the person focus upon what you are saying as they will hear how they can improve. If you don't have any constructive, specific or developmental follow-on points then don't create them just for the sake of it. Conversely, if you do have any negative points or criticisms, don't say '*my only negative point is…*' or '*my only criticisms are…*'. It's much better to replace these words and say '*some areas for development could be…*'.

You also need to make sure you are not being ambiguous or vague; you need to be factual regarding what you have seen and heard, not just give your personal opinion. Bear in mind that what you say can help or hinder a person's progress and confidence. Starting with something positive will help their motivation; they are then likely to listen to what else you have to say, which will aid their development. Starting with something negative can be demoralising and they may not listen to what else is said. Negative comments can have a more powerful impact than positive ones even though they are not nice to hear. If you do need to give negative feedback, always back this up with specific suggestions as to how the person can improve what they have done, rather than improve as a person.

Feedback should be a two-way process, allowing a discussion to take place to clarify any points. Consider your tone of voice and take into account any non-verbal signals, you may need to adapt your feedback if you see someone is becoming uncomfortable. Be aware of your own body language, facial expressions and tone of voice, and don't use confrontational words, or words likely to cause offence.

If you are writing feedback to be read at a later time; appreciate that *how* you write it may not be how it is read. It is easy to interpret words or phrases differently to those intended. Statements such as *well done* or *good* don't say *what* was *well done* or *good* or how it can be improved for the future. However, statements such as *your use of the technology was very effective and demonstrated the point very well – well done* makes the feedback more explicit.

If peer feedback is to be given after the micro-teach sessions, your observer should have planned who will be giving it and to whom, to enable everyone to focus carefully upon the relevant individual's session. The feedback you are giving is only your opinion: the observer will also be giving feedback and should clarify any points you have raised to ensure the person you have given feedback to does not feel demoralised. They may also give you feedback on how you have given feedback to your peers, to help you improve your own skills. If you can give feedback in a skilful manner, the others in the room will also learn from and benefit by what you have said. Peer assessment and constructive feedback has a valuable contribution to make to everyone's learning and development within the group.

Receiving feedback

Once you have finished your micro-teach session, you might be so relieved or busy packing away that you don't fully take on board what is being said to you. Listen carefully to your observer, and ask questions to clarify any points you are unsure of. Try not to interrupt or become defensive when receiving feedback and don't take anything personally – the feedback will be given to help you improve.

Receiving feedback can sometimes be difficult as people often think it will be negative or critical. If one of your peers gives you negative feedback you might feel your self-esteem is in question and want to be defensive or argumentative. If this happens, listen to what they say, but remember it is their opinion, and your observer will also give you feedback which may differ from this. Just say *'I'll take your comments on board'* rather than arguing. Conversely, you might receive really good feedback and not know how to react. If this is the case, simply say *'thank you for your comments'*.

When receiving feedback, whether from your observer or your peers, you need to listen carefully, focusing on the positive as well as any negative or constructive points. The feedback from your observer should be given skilfully to help you realise what you did well and what you could improve upon for the future to reach your full potential as a teacher or trainer.

You should receive a completed feedback form or checklist from your observer, and possibly from your peers; these can be used to inform your self-evaluation process.

Evaluating your session

Evaluating your delivery is an important aspect of your own learning and development and you may need to complete a self-evaluation form to formalise this. You might think you have done really well, but you might receive some helpful advice during the feedback process which could help you improve further.

After your session you may find that your observer will ask you how you felt it went before giving you feedback. This will enable you to consider what went well and what you could have done differently. You should receive oral feedback along with written feedback such as a completed observation report or checklist.

When evaluating yourself, consider your strengths, areas for development and any action and improvements required from a teaching perspective as well as your subject knowledge.

Some questions to ask yourself include:

- how did I feel after I delivered my session?
- did I achieve my aim?
- did the learners achieve the objectives?
- what are my strengths and areas for development?
- did I deliver within the time or did I have to adjust/change anything?
- did I engage and include all my learners throughout the session?
- how effective were the teaching, learning and assessment approaches I used?
- how did I know how much learning took place by each learner?
- how did my session meet the needs of the group and individuals?
- did anything go wrong – if so what did I do, or could I do in the future to ensure this does not happen again?
- what would I do differently next time and why?
- how can I use the feedback received to improve for the future?

Hopefully, you enjoyed your micro-teach session and it has confirmed you do want to have a career as a teacher or trainer. However, the experience might have made you think that it just isn't for you at this point in time. Conversely it might make you more determined to improve and develop further.

Micro-teach checklist

You might like to use this checklist to help you plan and deliver your micro-teach session.

Before

☐ Decide on a topic that you feel knowledgeable about and confident to deliver, and one that is suitable to your group. Try not to change your mind too often about what you plan to deliver

☐ Find out how many learners you will be delivering to, their learning preferences (if possible) and any particular needs they may have

□ Find out when and where you will be delivering, at what time and for how long

□ Prepare your plan in advance, ensuring you have a clear aim (what you want your learners to achieve) and SMART objectives (how they will achieve your aim, e.g. demonstrate, describe, explain). It would be useful to ask your observer to comment on your plan beforehand

□ Plan what will be covered during the beginning, middle and ending sections of your session, and allocate timings to each activity. You need to keep your learners engaged, active and motivated so that the session is focused upon their learning

□ Keep things simple – don't try to achieve too much as time will go quickly; equally, don't expect too much from your learners as they might be new to your topic

□ Prepare an extra activity in case you have spare time

□ Know what you can reduce or remove if you run short of time

□ Prepare all your resources, check for spelling, grammar, punctuation and sentence construction errors in handouts and presentations. If you use pictures, make sure they positively represent all aspects of equality and diversity. Check you are not infringing copyright in any way, and reference any text you have used from books, journals or the internet

□ Rehearse your session in front of friends or family to check your timings

□ Plan ahead – practise using the relevant technology, equipment and/or resources beforehand

□ Photocopy handouts and materials as required, book equipment if necessary

□ Have a contingency plan in case something goes wrong or isn't available

□ Have spare pens, paper, etc.

□ Check if you can arrive early to prepare the room, equipment and resources

During

□ Set up the area to suit your topic, so that all learners can see and hear you

□ Have a watch or clock handy to keep track of the time

□ Keep your session plan in view so that you can look at it when necessary to make sure you are on track with your timing

□ Relax, take a few deep breaths and focus on what you are going to do. Leave all personal issues behind

□ When you start, smile and use eye contact with everyone, introduce yourself, your topic and your aim

□ State the objectives clearly and/or have them written down somewhere for referring back to at the end

□ Check for prior knowledge and/or experience and draw on this throughout your session (go from the *known* to the *unknown*)

☐ Speak a little slower and louder than normal

☐ Deliver your topic confidently, remaining focused, staying in control, acting professionally and trying to relax while enjoying the experience

☐ Engage your learners, project energy, enthusiasm and passion for your subject

☐ Pace the session according to your learners, involve them so the session is centred around them and not you, differentiate activities as necessary and take into account any learner needs

☐ Make sure you involve every learner at some point during your delivery, i.e. use their names, ask an individual question, and use eye contact

☐ Limit the use of jargon and acronyms, and explain each one when used

☐ Ask open questions to test knowledge and understanding (ones that begin with *who, what, when, where, why* and *how*)

☐ Check learning has taken place by carrying out some form of assessment activity, for example, observation, written or oral questions

☐ If you set a group activity, think about what you will be doing while your learners are active, give a target time for completion

☐ Always confirm achievement (or otherwise) to each individual, and give constructive feedback

☐ At the end of your session, allow time for questions from your learners, but keep an eye on the time as you could easily overrun

☐ When summarising, recap your aim and the objectives

☐ It is useful to provide a handout to summarise your topic with further information, for example, text books, websites, etc.

☐ If you are unsure how to end your session, simply say '*Thank you, I've enjoyed my session with you today*'

Afterwards

☐ Tidy the area

☐ Listen to the feedback from your observer (and peers if applicable)

☐ Don't be annoyed with yourself if you made any mistakes: the micro-teach session is a developmental learning opportunity

☐ Evaluate what went well and why, and what didn't go well and why, and take into consideration the feedback you have received

☐ Make sure you complete any required documentation and submit it by the target date

Summary

In this chapter you have learnt about:

- *the micro-teach session*
- *planning to deliver your session*
- *facilitating your session*
- *assessing learning*
- *giving and receiving feedback*
- *evaluating your session*
- *the micro-teach checklist*

Theory focus

References and further information

Duckworth, V, Wood, J, Bostock, J and Dickinson, J (2010) *Successful Teaching Practice in the Lifelong Learning Sector.* Exeter: Learning Matters.

Gravells, A (2013) *The Award in Education and Training.* London: Learning Matters SAGE.

Websites

Assessment resources – www.excellencegateway.org.uk

Education and Training Foundation – http://www.et-foundation.co.uk

Giving feedback – www.brookes.ac.uk/services/ocsld/firstwords/fw21.html

Learning preferences questionnaire – www.vark-learn.com

Oxford Learning Institute – Giving and receiving feedback – http://tinyurl.com/688tfev

Video regarding micro teaching by Ann Gravells – http://www.maketiny.co.uk/J27831E

APPENDIX 1

Educational abbreviations and acronyms

ACL	Adult and Community Learning
ADD	Attention Deficit Disorder
ADHD	Attention Deficit and Hyperactivity Disorder
ADS	Adult Dyslexia Support
AELP	Association of Employment and Learning Providers
AI	Awarding Institution
AO	Awarding Organisation
AoC	Association of Colleges
ASD	Autism Spectrum Disorder
ATL	Association of Teachers and Lecturers
ATLS	Associate Teacher Learning and Skills
BEd	Bachelor of Education
BIS	Department for Business, Innovation and Skills
BME	Black and Minority Ethnic
CAVTL	Commission on Adult Vocational Teaching and Learning
CCEA	Council for the Curriculum, Examinations and Assessment (Northern Ireland)
CETT	Centre for Excellence in Teacher Training
Cert Ed	Certificate in Education
CL	Community Learning
CLA	Copyright Licensing Authority
COSHH	Control of Substances Hazardous to Health
CPD	Continuing Professional Development
CQFW	Credit and Qualification Framework for Wales
CRB	Criminal Records Bureau
DBS	Disclosure and Barring Service
DCELLS	Department for Children, Education, Lifelong Learning and Skills (Wales)
DSO	Designated Safeguarding Officer
E&D	Equality and Diversity
EBD	Emotional and Behavioural Difficulties
ECDL	European Computer Driving Licence
EDAR	Experience, Describe, Analyse and Revise
EDIP	Explain, Demonstrate, Imitate and Practise
EI	Emotional Intelligence
EHRC	Equality and Human Rights Commission
ESOL	English for Speakers of Other Languages
EQA	External Quality Assurance
FAQ	Frequently Asked Questions
FE	Further Education
FHE	Further and Higher Education
GCSE	General Certificate of Secondary Education
GLH	Guided Learning Hours
H&S	Health and Safety
HEA	Higher Education Academy
HEI	Higher Education Institution
IAG	Information, Advice and Guidance
IAP	Individual Action Plan
ICT	Information and Communication Technology
IfL	Institute for Learning
IIP	Investors in People
ILA	Individual Learning Account

(Continued)

(Continued)

ILP	Individual Learning Plan
ILT	Information and Learning Technology
IT	Information Technology
ITE	Initial Teacher Education
ITP	Independent Training Provider
ISA	Independent Safeguarding Authority
ITT	Initial Teacher/Trainer Training
IQ	Intelligence Quotient
IQA	Internal Quality Assurance
IWB	Interactive Whiteboard
LA	Local Authority
LAR	Learner Achievement Record
LDD	Learning Difficulties and/or Disabilities
LLUK	Lifelong Learning UK (no longer operational)
LSA	Learner Support Assistant
LSIS	Learning and Skills Improvement Service (no longer operational)
LSCB	Local Safeguarding Children Board
MLD	Moderate Learning Difficulties
MOODLE	Modular Object-Oriented Dynamic Learning Environment
NEET	Not in Education, Employment or Training
NIACE	National Institute of Adult Continuing Education
NLH	Notional Learning Hours
NOS	National Occupational Standards
NQT	Newly Qualified Teacher
NRDC	National Research and Development Centre for Adult Literacy and Numeracy
NTA	Non-teaching Assistant
NVQ	National Vocational Qualification
Ofqual	Office of Qualifications and Examinations Regulation
Ofsted	Office for Standards in Education, Children's Services and Skills
PAT	Portable Appliance Testing
PCET	Post Compulsory Education and Training
PGCE	Post Graduate Certificate in Education
PLTS	Personal Learning and Thinking Skills
POCA	Protection of Children Act (1999)
PPP	Pose, Pause, Pick
PSHE	Personal, Social and Health Education
QCF	Qualifications and Credit Framework
QTLS	Qualified Teacher Learning and Skills
QTS	Qualified Teacher Status (schools)
RLJ	Reflective Learning Journal
RPL	Recognition of Prior Learning
RWE	Realistic Working Environment
SEAL	Social and Emotional Aspects of Learning
SCN	Scottish Candidate Number
SCQF	Scottish Credit and Qualifications Framework
SfA	Skills Funding Agency
SL	Student Loan
SLC	Subject Learning Coach
SMART	Specific, Measurable, Achievable, Relevant and Timebound
SoW	Scheme of Work
SP	Session Plan
SSB	Standard Setting Body
SSC	Sector Skills Council
SWOT	Strengths, Weaknesses, Opportunities and Threats
T&L	Teaching and Learning
TAQA	Training, Assessment and Quality Assurance
UCU	University and College Union
ULN	Unique Learner Number
VACSR	Valid, Authentic, Current, Sufficient and Reliable
VARK	Visual, Aural, Read/write and Kinaesthetic
VB	Vetting and Barring
VLE	Virtual Learning Environment
WBL	Work Based Learning
WEA	Workers' Educational Association
WWWWWH	Who, What, When, Where, Why and How

Glossary of educational terms

Term	Definition
Accredited	A qualification leading to a recognised certificate issued by an awarding organisation.
Action Plan	A formal agreement between a teacher and a learner agreeing what will be achieved with target dates.
Activity	A short task designed to enable learners to consolidate their learning.
Aim	A general statement outlining what the teacher hopes to achieve with their learners.
Andragogy	Learner-centred process where the learners take control of the learning process, as opposed to learning which is totally led by the teacher.
Assessment	A way of finding out if learning has taken place.
Assessment cycle	The full process of assessment from beginning to end.
Assessment criteria	Statements used in the Qualification Credit Framework (QCF) to determine what learners can do.
Assessment method	A way of finding out if learning has taken place, e.g. assignment, observation, questions, etc.
Assessment plan	A formal individual agreement of what will be assessed, when and where, often updated for the assessment of different units or aspects over time.
Assessment type	A style of assessment, e.g. initial, formative, summative, etc.
Assessor	Person responsible for making a decision about a learner's achievements.
Attention span	The amount of time a learner can concentrate without being distracted.
Authentic	Something that's genuine, i.e. all the learner's own work.
Award	A term used in the QCF to denote a qualification with 12 credits or fewer.
Awarding organisation	An organisation recognised by Ofqual for the purpose of awarding qualifications to learners.
Barriers to learning	Concerns or issues that could hinder learning taking place, e.g. transport, English as a second language, etc.

(Continued)

(Continued)

Term	Definition
Benchmarking	A way of evaluating learner performance against an accepted standard once a standard is set, it can be used as a basis for the expectation of achievements with other groups and/or learners.
Blended learning	Using more than one method of teaching and learning, usually including technology.
Boundaries	Restrictions affecting teaching or learning, i.e. the role of the teacher, not overstepping their responsibilities.
Buddy	Another learner on the same programme who can give support.
Centre	A registered training provider responsible for administering programmes which are accredited by an awarding organisation.
Certificate	A term used in the QCF to denote a qualification with 13-36 credits.
Communication	The transfer of information from one person to another, with the intention of bringing about a response.
Contact time	Time spent in contact with a teacher or assessor who is guiding the learning process.
Continuing professional development (CPD)	The process of keeping up to date with relevant subject knowledge and experience.
Credit	One credit on the Qualifications and Credit Framework equates to ten notional hours of learning.
Current	Up to date.
Diagnostic assessment	A way of ascertaining a learner's current skills and knowledge towards a particular subject.
Differentiation	Recognising differences in people. Amending activities to cater for different levels of learner.
Diploma	A term used in the QCF to denote a qualification with 37 or more credits.
Discrimination	Showing favouritism, bias, prejudice, intolerance or unfairness to others without just cause.
Distance learning	Learning which takes place away from the organisation offering the programme/qualification.
Diversity	Valuing individual differences.
Energiser	Fun and light hearted activities to energise learners, e.g. after a lunch break. Similar to icebreakers but carried out with learners who already know each other.
Engage	Encouraging learner interaction and involvement with others.
Equality	Having equal rights regardless of age, gender, sexual orientation, etc.
Evaluation	Measuring the effectiveness of a session or a programme of learning.
Evidence	Proof of learner achievement, e.g. written statements, work products, etc.

Term	Definition
External quality assurance	A process carried out by a person accountable to the awarding organisation who carries out quality assurance of organisations offering qualifications.
Feedback	Information given to learners to confirm achievement, give support and/or motivate.
Formal	A recognised way of doing something, i.e. formal assessment might include a test issued by an awarding organisation.
Formative	Ongoing, i.e. assessment on an ongoing basis rather than at the end of a subject or course.
Ground rules	Agreed codes of behaviour between the teacher and the learner. Usually agreed at the beginning of the programme, e.g. not using mobile phones.
Holistic	Covering several aspects at the same time, e.g. delivering or assessing more than one aspect of a qualification.
Icebreaker	Fun and light hearted ways of introducing learners to each other – usually carried out at the commencement of a course.
Inclusive	Involving everyone, treating them equally and fairly.
Induction	The process carried out at the beginning of a course to ensure learners receive all the required information.
Informal	Carrying out something in addition to what is required, i.e. informal assessment might be a quiz to test knowledge in a fun way.
Information and communication technology (ICT)	Ways of using computers and modern technology, e.g. e-mail, word processing, presentations, searching the internet, etc.
Initial assessment	Assessment carried out at the beginning of a programme or session to ascertain prior knowledge and skills.
In-service	Currently in a teaching or training role.
Interactive whiteboard	An electronic board used to display information and presentations which can be connected to the internet.
Internal quality assurance	A process carried out by a person accountable to the organisation to monitor and sample aspects of the learner journey from commencement to completion.
Learner	A person taking a learning programme, can also be called a candidate, student, trainee, depending upon the context in which learning takes place.
Learning environment	Anywhere learning takes place, it can include classrooms, workshops, training rooms, prisons, the outdoors, etc.
Learning journal	An ongoing diary to note incidents and how they were dealt with, focusing on how to improve as a result.
Learning outcome	Statements used in the QCF to determine what learners will do.
Learning preferences	A particular way in which an individual prefers to learn, e.g. visual, aural, read/write and kinaesthetic (VARK).

(Continued)

(Continued)

Term	Definition
Level	A measure of the demand of a qualification. QCF levels start at Entry and go up to 8 in England (12 in Scotland).
Mentor	Person giving one-to-one support who is skilled and/or knowledgeable in the same subject area as the learner.
Micro-teach session	A short formal delivery of a session followed by an evaluation of practice.
Minimum core	Literacy, language, numeracy and ICT – the minimum skills a teacher should demonstrate.
Motivation	Factors influencing a learner's learning, e.g. intrinsic – the desire to learn for own self-fulfilment, and/or extrinsic – external factors such as a pay rise at work or the achievement of a qualification.
Non-accredited	A course which does not lead to a formal qualification.
Non-contact time	Time spent not in contact with a teacher or assessor, i.e. for homework, studies, assignment work, research, etc.
Non-verbal communication	Any communication that does not involve the spoken word, e.g. body language, facial expression.
Objective	Explicit ways in which learners can achieve the teacher's aim, e.g. by demonstrating, describing, explaining, etc. Objectives should be achieveable and measureable to assess that learning has taking place.
One to one	Teaching or training with one learner rather than a group.
Pedagogy	Teacher-centred process where the teacher leads the learning rather than the learner.
Peer assessment	Assessment by other learners or colleagues in the same peer group.
Peer feedback	Feedback given to learners by learners.
Plagiarism	Copying the work of someone else without acknowledging or referencing the source.
Points of referral	People or places to refer a learner to if necessary.
Pralse sandwich	A method of giving feedback by sandwiching areas for development/negative points within positive aspects.
Pre-service	Not yet in a teaching or training role.
Process	Teaching additional relevant topics, besides what is stated in the qualification or programme.
Product	Only teaching the minimum requirements as stated in the qualification or programme.
Programme of learning	A structured course which might or might not be accredited by an awarding organisation.
Progression	Developing further after achievement, e.g. taking a level 3 qualification after achieving a level 2.
Qualification	A formally recognised programme of learning leading to a certificate issued by an awarding organisation.

Term	Definition
Qualifications and credit framework (QCF)	A system for recognising skills and qualifications in England (SCQF in Scotland and CQFW in Wales).
Qualitative	Quality information obtained by open questions, reports, surveys and discussions.
Quality Assurance	Organisational audit procedures (internal and external) to ensure standards are maintained.
Quantitative	Quantity information, e.g. data and statistics obtained by closed questions, results from tests and other data gathering techniques.
Reasonable adjustments	Amendments which can be made regarding assessment of learners to meet their particular needs. They are usually agreed in advance with the awarding organisation.
Record of achievement	Formal recognition of achievement listing what was achieved; might not necessarily be accredited by an awarding organisation, but could be issued in-house.
Record of attendance	Proof of attendance at an event but not proof of achievement.
Records	Documents used to support the teaching and learning process which satisfy internal and external requirements.
Refer	To direct a learner to other people or agencies who can help with a concern they may have to give a learner another chance to achieve, i.e. if they haven't passed first time but have not failed the activity.
Referencing	Acknowledging the sources of reading and research within work.
Reflection	Thinking about what has occurred, what can be improved and analysing why.
Reliable	Consistent.
Resources	Materials used to enhance the learning process, e.g. handouts, computers, text books, audio visual equipment, etc.
Safeguarding	Ensuring the protection and safety of learners.
Self-assessment	Assessment by the learner of their own progress and achievement.
Scheme of Work	An outline of what will be covered during a programme of learning.
Session Plan	An outline of what will be covered during a session with learners – also known as a teaching and learning plan.
Standardisation	Ensuring your practice is consistent with others.
Subjective	A personal decision rather than an objective decision, i.e. where the assessment criteria might not be clearly stated, it can be unfair to the learner as they might not be aware of what is required.
Sufficient	Enough, i.e. sufficient work has been provided by the learner to meet the requirements.
Summative	At the end, i.e. assessment at the end of a topic rather than on an ongoing basis.

(Continued)

(Continued)

Term	Definition
Teacher	Generic term for trainer, tutor, instructor, facilitator, lecturer, i.e. someone who enables learning to take place.
Teaching and learning approaches	Methods of facilitating learning, e.g. discussion, e-learning, presentation, project, group work, etc.
Teaching and learning plan	An outline of what will be covered during a session with learners – also known as a session plan.
Teaching, learning and assessment cycle	Systematic approach to teaching and learning in five stages: identifying needs, planning learning, facilitating learning, assessing learning, and evaluation. Quality assurance should run throughout and everything should focus on the learner and the learning taking place.
Unit	A module or component of learning which is expressed as learning outcomes and assessment criteria in the QCF. All units have a level, title and credit value; for example, The Level 3 Award in Education and Training is three credits. Units can be achieved on their own, or as part of a qualification.
Valid	Suitable, i.e. a valid assessment only assesses what should be assessed, not other aspects which are not relevant.

Qualification structure for the Level 3 Award in Education and Training (12 credits)

The Award in Education and Training is made up of the following three units (which total 12 credits):

- Understanding, roles, responsibilities and relationships in education and training (3 credits)
- Understanding and using inclusive teaching and learning approaches in education and training (6 credits)
- Understanding assessment in education and training (3 credits)

However, it is possible to achieve part of the Award by taking units from the Learning and Development qualification (see the table below). These units are known as *accepted equivalents*, but they are only for those who are currently in a teaching and assessing role with learners of their own:

- Facilitate learning and development for individuals (6 credits) OR
- Facilitate learning and development in groups (6 credits)
- Understanding the principles and practices of assessment (3 credits)

Group A This 3 credit unit is mandatory	Understanding roles, responsibilities and relationships in education and training *(3 credits Education and Training unit)*		
Group B One unit (6 credits) must be achieved from this group	Understanding and using inclusive teaching and learning approaches in education and training *(6 credits Education and Training unit)*	Facilitate learning and development for individuals *(6 credits Learning and Development unit)*	Facilitate learning and development in groups *(6 credits Learning and Development unit)*
Group C One unit (3 credits) must be achieved from this group	Understanding assessment in education and training *(3 credits Education and Training unit)*	Understanding the principles and practices of assessment *(3 credits Learning and Development unit)*	

INDEX